THE
FIBRE
FIX

THE
FIBRE
FIX

How to Eat More Fibre to
Supercharge Your Health

KRISTEN STAVRIDIS

First published 2026 by Bluebird
an imprint of Pan Macmillan
The Smithson, 6 Briset Street, London EC1M 5NR
EU representative: Macmillan Publishers Ireland Ltd, 1st Floor,
The Liffey Trust Centre, 117–126 Sheriff Street Upper, Dublin 1, D01 YC43
Associated companies throughout the world

ISBN 978-1-0350-8709-9

Copyright © Kristen Stavridis 2026

The right of Kristen Stavridis to be identified as the author of this work has been asserted in accordance with the Copyright, Designs and Patents Act 1988.

All rights reserved. No part of this publication may be reproduced, stored in a retrieval system, or transmitted, in any form, or by any means (including, without limitation, electronic, mechanical, photocopying, recording or otherwise) without the prior written permission of the publisher.

Pan Macmillan does not have any control over, or any responsibility for, any author or third-party websites (including, without limitation, URLs, emails and QR codes) referred to in or on this book.

1 3 5 7 9 8 6 4 2

A CIP catalogue record for this book is available from the British Library.

Typeset by Heather Bowen
Printed and bound in the UK using 100% Renewable Electricity by CPI Group (UK) Ltd

This book contains the opinions and ideas of its author. It is intended to provide helpful general information on the subjects that it addresses. It is not in any way a substitute for the advice of the reader's own physician(s) or other medical professionals based on the reader's own individual conditions, symptoms, or concerns. If the reader needs personal medical, health, dietary, exercise, or other assistance or advice, the reader should consult a competent physician and/ or other qualified health care professionals. The author and publisher specifically disclaim all responsibility for injury, damage, or loss that the reader may incur as a direct or indirect consequence of following any directions or suggestions given in the book or participating in any programmes described in the book. The reader is advised not to undertake, cease, or modify any treatments, diets, or health procedures without consulting a professional. Failure to adhere to this recommendation may result in adverse health impacts, for which the author and publisher accept no responsibility.

This book is sold subject to the condition that it shall not, by way of trade or otherwise, be lent, hired out, or otherwise circulated without the publisher's prior consent in any form of binding or cover other than that in which it is published and without a similar condition including this condition being imposed on the subsequent purchaser. The publisher does not authorize the use or reproduction of any part of this book in any manner for the purpose of training artificial intelligence technologies or systems. The publisher expressly reserves this book from the Text and Data Mining exception in accordance with Article 4(3) of the European UnionDigital Single Market Directive 2019/790.

Visit **www.panmacmillan.com/bluebird** to read more about
all our books and to buy them.

Whether you are well-versed in fibre's 'super-nutrient' status, or you are completely new to its endless benefits, this book is for you. Because no matter who we are, we could all benefit from eating a little more fibre and knowing just how much it can transform our health.

Contents

Introduction 1

PART 1
Fibre Foundations

Chapter 1: Let's Chat Fibre 9
Chapter 2: Fibre's Benefits 15
Chapter 3: Fibre and the Gut 35
Chapter 4: Fibre is Key to Preventing Disease 47
Chapter 5: Why Are We Ghosting the Good Stuff? ... 59

PART 2
How to Make Fibre Your Superpower

Six Steps to 30g 73
Step 1: What to Know Before You Start 74
Step 2: Re-shape Your Plate to Boost Fibre 80
Step 3: Get Your Fibre Fix – What to Eat 87
Step 4: Perfect Your Plant Points 118
Step 5: Overcoming Fibre Frustrations 124
Step 6: Stay on Top of Your Fibre Game 130

PART 3
Recipes and Meal Plans

Breakfast	**141**
Main Dishes	**149**
Snacks	**167**
Sides and Condiments	**173**
Sweet Treats	**181**
Meal Plans	**189**
Flexi Meal Plan 1	190
Flexi Meal Plan 2	192
Vegetarian Meal Plan	194
Vegan Meal Plan	196
Supplements 101	199
Endnotes	205
Acknowledgements	218
Index	220

Introduction

Discover the secret to losing weight, looking younger and feeling better than ever: FIBRE.

P icture this: You're healthy. Your skin is glowing. You have more energy than ever before. You no longer feel sluggish, and your bloating is *finally* under control. Weight is coming off more easily, and you feel 'regular' again. All because you began to incorporate more of one specific super-nutrient into your diet.

This super-nutrient is called 'fibre', and for years it has been overlooked and underestimated in terms of its health-boosting powers. Until now. This book aims to bring fibre back into the spotlight, changing the way you think about fibre forever and showing you just how life-changing it can be for you to add more into your diet. As you dive into this book, you may be excited to get started straight away with the recipes and meal plans in Part 3, but I recommend you read Parts 1 and 2 first. Not only will these sections give you a chance to get well-versed with all the benefits of the fibre you are eating, it will also motivate you to increase the amount of fibre you are currently eating and stick to it long term. In Part 2 there is also very important information that everyone needs to know regarding how exactly you should increase your intake – too much, too fast, and without adequate water intake, can often lead to pesky unwanted symptoms, such as bloating or gas.

How fibre changed my life
My own story with fibre is part of the reason I really wanted to write this book. Towards the end of 2021, I was struggling with my health and spent most of the time feeling groggy, sluggish, bloated and just generally unwell. I had gained weight, my face had broken out in acne that wouldn't budge, and I was struggling with my mental health. Up to this point, I had tried so many different things – supplements, cleanses, fasting, gluten-free diet, dairy-free diet, you name it – but nothing was working. And it was not just affecting me physically: I felt like the brain fog was taking over, too, which was affecting my career. I had also stopped ovulating, and my menstrual cycle was all over the place. I wanted to hide, feeling so much shame to be experiencing all these symptoms for so long when I was a nutritionist and was meant to be the vision of health.

I decided to get back to the drawing board and go back to basics. I remembered an online seminar I had attended one year prior which was centred around 'gut health'. Gut health was becoming the next big thing in the health space, with a huge number of studies being funded and groundbreaking research being shared every minute. I knew that our gut was connected to so many different systems – brain health, immune health, skin health and more – and it was like a light was switched on in my head. That was my answer. I needed to focus *specifically* on my gut.

I knew that one of the most important things that our gut needed to function optimally was the often-overlooked nutrient, fibre. Admittedly, over those past few months I had been falling *very* short on it. Due to my symptoms and weight gain, I had been eating a very high-protein and low-carbohydrate diet, but things just seemed to be getting worse. I was not properly looking after myself, and the number of plants I was eating was pretty low, as I had thought that they were worsening my gut symptoms.

I set out to do a complete turnaround and focused on filling my diet with more nutritious plant foods, while boosting my fibre intake slowly but surely to support my health. The results after a few weeks were astronomical. My skin cleared up for the first time in months. I felt confident leaving the house without makeup. The uncomfortable bloating, which felt like it was taking over my life after I ate anything, had reduced. My energy levels were boosted, I was ovulating again, the brain fog cleared, I looked less inflamed and puffy, and my mental health was much, *much* better. I felt like I was myself again after struggling for so long.

After going from eating 14–16g of fibre per day, I was consistently eating 35–40g per day. This boost in fibre intake felt like it had been *exactly* what my gut had needed, cleaning me up from the inside out and helping kickstart my digestion and get my gut bacteria back to where it should have been. I felt like I had a new body. I decided to make it my *mission* to help as many people who suffered the same symptoms I had experienced as I could.

Since then, I have worked with hundreds of people all over the world with my gut health programme (which mainly helped people boost their diet quality and get more fibre into their diet), while also sharing as much of this life-changing information with as many people as possible through in-person talks as well as social media. I want to show everyone how much fibre can transform their health, and I am excited to be sharing all my knowledge with you in this book. I am so confident in fibre's life-changing benefits that I even conducted a six-week experiment on myself (see page 45) to demonstrate to you the difference it can make to our health.

What actually *is* fibre?
Fibre is the indigestible part of plants and foods like wholegrains that makes up a lot of their cellular structure. Most people associate fibre with foods like bran flakes and prunes, but what if I told you that you can also find fibre in foods like avocados, dark chocolate, baked beans, popcorn and nuts? I've mentioned that fibre is 'indigestible', so should we, and do we even need to be, eating it?! Well, as you will see in later sections of this book, that is **the whole point**. Many of the great benefits of fibre come from the fact that we *cannot* digest it (on our own, at least).

Doesn't fibre just help you poop?
One of the biggest misconceptions about fibre is that it only has one job: to prevent constipation. However, fibre is much, *much* more than that – it really is the unsung hero when it comes to so many aspects of our health. Want to lower your cholesterol? Fibre can help. Looking to boost your gut health? Eat more fibre. Looking to support your mental health? You've got it – fibre. Fibre may also add years to our lives[1], play a role in helping our bodies fight off infection and even reduce our risk of developing killer diseases. In fact, it has been shown that a 7–10g increase in the amount of fibre you eat daily can reduce your risk of developing cardiovascular disease by 9%[2], colorectal cancer by 10%[3], stroke by 7%[4] and type 2 diabetes by 6%[5]. What if I told you that consuming more fibre

could also boost brain power[6,7,8], is associated with a lower risk of developing things like dementia[9] and Parkinson's[10] disease and can even help you lose weight[11], too? Fibre is responsible for *so* much more than we realize.

But right now, we are living through a big fibre crisis. Over **90% of people in the UK and USA are not getting enough in their diets every day**, which may contribute to the increase in many digestive disorders and life-threatening diseases. The fibre gap is huge. Fibre has been identified as a 'nutrient of concern' by the Dietary Guidelines for Americans since 2005, as well as a nutrient for which, year after year, most of the UK population fails to meet the recommended intake of. Our modern-day diets are filled with fibre-devoid ultra-processed foods and are very far from the plant-rich diets our ancestors used to eat. In fact, it has been estimated that our ancestors consumed as much as 100g of fibre per day[12] – a stark contrast to today's average of just 14–19g.

I want to show you just how *impressive* fibre is and how adding more of it to your diet can transform how you look and feel, as well as keeping you healthier for longer. So, if you are ready to make some big changes one small, fibre-filled bite at a time, then let's get started!

As we dive into Part 1, prepare for an array of evidence-based guidance that will really help you understand fibre as a super-nutrient on a whole new level. You will see how it plays a much bigger role in our wellbeing than most people realize, how it can help to prevent disease, as well as how our modern lifestyles have left so many of us falling short.

PART 1
FIBRE FOUNDATIONS

CHAPTER 1

Let's Chat Fibre

We know so far that fibre is indigestible and is found in all plants, but what is it made from exactly? Fibre is a type of **carbohydrate**, but unlike refined carbs (think cakes, confectionery and white bread) that we are told to eat in moderation, it's the kind of carb we need *more* of. Refined carbs tend to be stripped of their fibre content, can contain high levels of added sugar, and are linked with poor health outcomes when we eat too much of them. Unrefined carbohydrates, on the other hand, like brown rice, lentils and apples, boost our energy levels, provide an array of health-enhancing nutrients and are usually a great source of fibre.

Carbohydrates are made up of little sugar building blocks called 'monosaccharides'. Think of them as individual Lego bricks that can be linked together in many ways and patterns, to form different types of fibre. Some of these individual monosaccharide 'Lego' bricks can also link together to form 'disaccharides', 'polysaccharides' or 'oligosaccharides', depending on how many sugar units – or Lego building blocks – they contain.

Most carbohydrates are broken down well by the human body with the help of chewing and digestive enzymes like amylase, but fibre is different. Fibre cannot be broken down by the human body, so we require bacteria that live in our gut to break it down for us (I'll explain this in Chapter 3). Some people assume that because the human body cannot absorb or break down fibre, this means we should avoid it and it is unnecessary for us to eat. This could not be further from the truth. If you are looking to merely exist and survive, then by all means avoid fibre completely. But if you are looking to *thrive*, then fibre will help support your health by lowering disease risks, helping you feel and look great, as well as just generally contributing to a better quality of life.

When we talk about all the different types of fibre, they are usually divided into two simple categories: 'soluble' and 'insoluble'. Soluble fibre dissolves in water and is found in plant foods like the flesh of a kiwi, apples (not the skin), carrots, oats, beans and lentils. It is amazing at helping to draw water into the stool, softening it and making it easier to pass, and preventing constipation. Soluble fibre is also fascinating because of its ability to turn into a gel-like substance when in contact with water, helping to keep things moving along nicely through our digestive system.

Insoluble fibres do exactly what they say on the tin. They do not break down in water. Instead, they stay intact and act as a 'structure' for everything passing through the digestive system, especially in the last part of it, called the colon. This type of fibre can be found in things like skins of fruit and vegetables (think apples, pears and even kiwi skins), as well as foods like spinach, Brussels sprouts, aubergines, sweetcorn and berries.

SOLUBLE AND INSOLUBLE AT WORK

Chia seeds are a great example of an ingredient that boasts both soluble and insoluble fibres. Have you ever soaked chia seeds and noticed the gloopy, gel-like substance forming around the seed? This is mainly soluble fibre. The tough outer shell of the seed is insoluble fibre, which stays mostly intact as it travels through the digestive system.

Recent research shows that many different types of foods contain a combination of both soluble and insoluble fibre, so classifying fibre into just two categories may be oversimplifying things. Scientists claim that fibre is not just soluble or insoluble, but should instead be classified based on characteristics like its 'viscosity' (thickness and stickiness) and 'fermentability'[13] (how well it can be broken down using the process of fermentation in the gut). However, to avoid getting too overwhelmed by the science, in this book we are going to stick to the two categories of fibre. Here are a few examples.

Types of fibre[14]

Pectins: Pectin is an example of soluble fibre that you can find in foods like lentils, apples and potatoes and is well fermented by our gut bacteria. Pectin is found in most plants, where it acts as a sort of 'glue' that sticks everything together (this is why it's great for adding to homemade jams and jellies). You may also see many gut health supplements made using or containing apple pectin if you check the labels on the packaging.

Cellulose: This is an insoluble fibre that passes through our digestive tract and adds bulk[15] and structure to stools, helping to prevent constipation. You may remember the word 'cellulose' from science class as a child as it makes up the structure of plant cell walls we all learnt about, giving them their 'rigidity'. You can find cellulose in plants, particularly green fruit and vegetables like spinach, celery and green apples, as well as flaxseeds.

Inulin: Inulin has become a popular fibre supplement in the health space in recent years. As a prebiotic fibre, it has a positive effect on our gut health by boosting beneficial gut bacteria that support digestion and produce health-supporting compounds called short-chain fatty acids (more about this on page 40). Inulin fibre consumption may also help to reduce some inflammation in the body. Try adding more leeks, Jerusalem artichokes and asparagus to your diet.

Beta-glucans: Beta-glucans are soluble fibres that have been associated with supporting heart health[16], lowering cholesterol[17] and even supporting our immune system, too[18], and are currently getting a lot of attention in the research world. Beta-glucans also act as a 'prebiotic', feeding the beneficial bacteria in your gut, and can be found in foods like oats and barley.

Resistant starch: Although not technically a fibre, resistant starch is included by many in the fibre category because it displays similar traits. Resistant starches resist digestion in the small intestine, but then go on to be fermented (meaning bacteria break them down and produce things like gases) in the colon by our helpful gut bacteria. This is beneficial to our health. I am a big fan of resistant starch because not only can it be found in foods naturally, such as green bananas, beans and lentils, but we can also increase how much of it is in certain foods during cooking and cooling processes.

BOOSTING RESISTANT STARCH

If you cook starchy foods like white potatoes or pasta, allow them to cool and reheat them later: this process can boost the resistant starch content. Rice is another great source of resistant starch when you allow it to completely cool before refrigerating and reheating it until steaming hot. In fact, one study demonstrated that when rice was cooked then cooled, it had over two times more resistant starch in it compared to rice that was consumed without cooling it first[19]. This increase in resistant starch can help control blood sugar levels and help us feel fuller for longer post-meals.

Gums: Gums are types of fibre that will dissolve in water (soluble fibre). You may find different types of gums such as guar gum (which comes from the seed of the Guar plant), xanthan gum (produced from sugars by a process of fermentation) or gum arabic (which comes from the sap oozing from acacia trees), in food products like yoghurt, condiments and ice cream, or in supplements to help with texture and stabilizing. They can help regulate blood sugar levels as well as lower bad cholesterol in the body.

Lignins: This insoluble fibre passes through the digestive system without being broken down or fermented by gut bacteria. It helps waste products pass through the digestive system efficiently and helps to prevent constipation, while also helping trigger mucous secretion in the colon, which helps to aid digestion and acts as a protective barrier. You can find it in foods like flaxseeds, nuts and green bananas.

PREBIOTIC FIBRE

When we talk about the different types of fibre, it is important to know that some, but not all, have special abilities to help our gut bugs produce health-boosting molecules or 'metabolites'. These fibres are called 'prebiotic fibres' and act as something for the bacteria that lives in our large intestine to feed on. Resistant starches, inulin, many gums, beta-glucans and pectins all count as prebiotic, supporting the health and growth of our gut bugs, whereas cellulose and lignin, for example, are not prebiotic and simply pass through the digestive system, helping to support gut motility – the process by which food moves through our digestive tract. I always say to clients that much of the fibre they eat isn't food for us, it is actually food for our gut bugs, keeping them happy and thriving and in return producing things like short-chain fatty acids (SCFAs), which can help reduce inflammation – but more about that in Chapter 3. You can find prebiotic fibres in foods like onions, garlic and cabbage.

CHAPTER 2

Fibre's Benefits

Up until around the 1970s, fibre was thought of simply as 'roughage', with not many functions other than to pass through the digestive system and help to prevent constipation. However, in 1970, scientific publications written by an Irish surgeon called Denis Burkitt – also commonly known then as 'The Fibre Man' – changed the course of fibre forever. Burkitt proposed that fibre had many other functions outside of just moving through our digestive system and bulking up our stools. He also hypothesized that low-fibre diets increased the risk of diseases like coronary heart disease, obesity, certain cancers, diabetes, disorders of the large bowel and more. Since then, there has been a re-awakening in the research around fibre, showing that indeed it has many more benefits to our health than we ever could have imagined. Despite the big shift and better-quality research around fibre, many of us are still not aware of how it can help us.

So, are you ready to take a closer look at fibre's health superpowers? In Chapter 4, I'll cover fibre's impact on disease prevention (first heralded by The Fibre Man), but first, keep reading to discover incredibly impressive feel-good benefits that you might find surprising.

The secret weight-loss hack nobody told you about

If you search for 'weight-loss hacks' on social media and online, you will find a wave of misinformation where people will make claims that all sorts of foods or fads are **THE** secret hack to weight loss. It can seem so overwhelming when it comes to where to start, what advice to listen to and what to completely avoid. For most people, creating a slight calorie deficit over a long period of time is the key to losing weight successfully, however, there is also another hack that is proven to support weight loss, especially when paired with a calorie deficit. What is this secret hack? Well, you probably guessed it: adding more fibre to your diet!

Research shows that eating a meal that is high in fibre can help you feel fuller for longer, potentially helping you snack less and reduce the amount you eat[20]. We also know that people who eat more fibre tend to weigh less and have less body fat[21], while individuals who consume a lower-fibre diet might be more likely to struggle with being overweight or being obese[22]. A study on women in the US showed that for every 1g increase in the fibre they ate over a 20-month period, their weight decreased by 0.25 kilos[23]. Pretty impressive, right? But not only that: in a study on 74,000 female nurses in the US it was seen that women with the highest intake of fibre gained about 1.5kg less than individuals with the lowest fibre intake. The high-fibre group also had a 49% less risk of major weight gain[24].

So, fibre proves to be effective for weight loss, especially when paired with a calorie deficit. One study on 176 men and women showed that increasing fibre using a supplement alongside a low-calorie diet over five weeks *significantly* improved weight loss compared to a placebo group who didn't receive a fibre supplement while doing the same diet [25].

But what is it about fibre that can help us with weight loss?

It boosts gut bacteria: When we eat a diet higher in certain types of soluble fibre, it can boost the diversity and ratios of certain gut bacteria. Having higher ratios of some types of bacteria (such as 'Prevotella') compared to others (such as 'Bacteroides') may make it easier for some people to lose body fat compared to others when on a higher-fibre and calorie-controlled diet[26].

It helps with the release of GLP-1 and other fullness hormones: Fibre can also boost the ability to increase the release of certain fullness hormones[27,28] like Peptide YY (PYY) and GLP-1, through the production of certain short-chain fatty acids from our gut bacteria. PYY is a hormone that is released by cells in both the small intestine and colon and reduces our appetite, while GLP-1 (which is also used in some weight-loss injections) has a similar effect and is released by cells in the gut and nerve cells in your brain stem. This reduction in appetite makes it easier to stay at a healthy weight.

Looking to lose weight while also keeping on top of your fibre game? Try starting your day with a bowl of porridge with added protein powder, chia seeds, raspberries and sunflower seeds. Not only will this kickstart your digestive system and start your day with over 10g of fibre (a third of what you need daily), it will also provide slow-releasing energy, to keep you feeling fuller for longer and therefore less likely to snack throughout the day.

It slows down the digestion process slightly: Fibre can also support weight loss by slowing down the rate at which food leaves your stomach – a process known as 'delayed gastric emptying' – meaning you feel fuller for longer. This feeling of fullness may also be down to how high-fibre foods generally take longer to be chewed, slowing down the speed at which we eat. This is great news for our digestive health, but also means that your body has more time to register that it is feeling full, meaning you can be less likely to overeat.

It helps you feel fuller for longer: We also see fibre's weight loss benefits because of its ability to expand as it passes through our system. Soluble fibre, found in foods like chia seeds, oats and apples, can bind water, leading to expansion when it hits the stomach and intestines, increasing the feeling of fullness and supporting weight loss. One randomized control trial showed that adding 8g of high-fibre banana flour (high in resistant starch) to a soup significantly reduced hunger levels and led to participants eating 14% fewer calories[29].

Fibre keeps things moving

We have mentioned a few times in this book how fibre can help keep things moving through the digestive system or 'gut' (more on this in Chapter 3). But why is this important? Well, think about the last time your diet was not as healthy as it could be. Perhaps you were travelling, you were out of your regular routine, or you were just so busy that your healthy eating patterns went out the window. Chances are that after a while you started to feel bloated, a little sluggish and you may have even felt a little 'backed up' or constipated. There are a lot of factors that could have made you feel this way, but it is likely that the lack of fibre you consumed during that time could have had a big impact.

When you are on holiday or travelling, start your day with fresh fruit such as kiwis, watermelon, blueberries, raspberries or strawberries. Not only do they taste delicious, and many are a good source of fibre, but they can also help with hydration (which is important to reduce constipation).

Fibre is the magical component in plants that will help add bulk to our stools, softening them by drawing more moisture in and helping them move through our system a lot more easily because it stimulates movement through your digestive system. This helps us eliminate any waste products in our body efficiently so that we feel more comfortable, and can play a role in helping to protect us from various diseases and ailments, such as colon cancer.

There are consistent research findings that show us the power of adding more fibre into our diets. One meta-analysis (this is a study of lots of different research studies), showed in fourteen studies that fibre supplementation, particularly pectin and psyllium fibre, significantly improved stool frequency (how often we go to the bathroom). The effects were most notable when the supplements were over 10g or more of fibre[30]. Another study that followed over ten thousand women in the UK for four years showed that for each 5g increment of fibre consumed per day, they reduced their odds of suffering with constipation by 12–16%[31]. There is also evidence that fibre can be beneficial for those suffering with IBS (irritable bowel syndrome), which in the UK affects around 13 million people[32] and between 25 and 45 million people in the United States[33]. Research to date shows us that soluble fibre can be more effective than insoluble fibre in relieving symptoms of IBS[34], but we know this can vary from person to person.

> **COULD BOOSTING FIBRE INTAKE SAVE THE ECONOMY?**
>
> Two studies – one from Canada and the other from the US – showed that there could be significant constipation-related cost savings when fibre intake was increased at a population level. The US study demonstrated that over $12 billion dollars could be saved each year in medical costs by increasing the amount of fibre in adults by 9g[35], while in Canada it was shown that if the population reached the adequate amounts of fibre needed daily, up to $31.9 million Canadian dollars could be saved in healthcare costs associated with constipation. Meanwhile, Bowel and Bladder UK shared that in the UK[36] between 2018 and 2019, £168 million was spent treating constipation, with £81 million of this including 'avoidable admissions to A&E'.

The blood sugar superhero

There has been a lot of focus on blood sugar in the media and online in recent years, in particular how to balance out blood sugar spikes. For healthy individuals, a little spike in blood sugar is normal after a meal. However, if you are eating a diet that is low in fibre and high in things like processed sugar, you may experience sharp rises and crashes in blood sugar, leading to you feeling more tired, cranky and sluggish. One of the best ways to keep your energy levels more consistent throughout the day and avoid blood sugar crashes is by adding more fibre into your meals, which can help slow down the absorption of glucose molecules. In more scientific terms, this is referred to as reducing the 'glycaemic response' of certain foods[37].

A simple way to reduce sharp blood sugar spikes and crashes is to pair higher-fibre carbohydrates with a source of protein and/or healthy fats. For example, instead of starting your day with a slice of white toast and honey (mainly carbohydrates), switch to a slice of wholemeal toast with a boiled egg and avocado. Or, if you usually start your day with a takeaway pastry and coffee from your local cafe, try switching it to a takeaway porridge pot with dried fruit and a small yoghurt on the side. Adding healthy fats and extra protein like this can help to slow down digestion and keep energy levels steadier.

Research shows that not eating enough fibre can increase your risk of developing diabetes[38, 39], as well as increasing your risk of something called 'insulin resistance'. Insulin is a hormone that is made by the body (specifically in the pancreas) which helps control how much sugar is in our blood. When somebody has 'insulin resistance', this means that cells in your body do not respond properly to this hormone, often leading to blood sugar levels getting a little out of control and even leading to weight gain in some people. One study published in 2012 by Cambridge University Press showed that women who consumed a high-fibre diet were 50% less likely to have insulin resistance than those who ate the least[40].

Fibre improves cognitive function

According to the American Psychological Association, cognitive function is what we call 'the performance of the mental processes of perception, learning, memory, understanding, awareness, reasoning, judgment, intuition, and language.' Having good cognitive function means that you can focus well, have good clarity of thought as well as memory, can communicate efficiently and can understand everyday things without confusion. For life to run smoothly, we want to ensure we are supporting our cognitive health, and this is where fibre can come in.

There are many ways to measure cognitive health, but research so far has given us an insight into some specific benefits in relation to high fibre consumption – from improving memory to helping your attention span. Researchers in the UK showed that during a 12-week study on twins, a daily fibre supplement helped improve visual memory and learning compared to placebo[41], while another study showed that people who ate more fibre from fruit and vegetables scored higher in tests demonstrating processing speed, attention, verbal fluency and memory[42]. Furthermore, in the same study on elderly people in the US, vegetable intake appeared to help people's ability to learn new verbal information, as well as helping with processing speed and sustained attention[43].

If you want to support your brain health and cognitive function, fibre is important – but not only as an adult. We now know that the amount of fibre you consume from as early as young adulthood can have an impact on cognitive function in middle age, potentially helping verbal learning and our memory[44]. So, loading up on extra portions of fruit and vegetables, adding beans and pulses to your plate and snacking on nuts and seeds while you're young will be one of the best hacks to help you feel sharp later in life. Dietary patterns that include a higher amount of fibre as well as antioxidants may be linked to **greater brain volume** and **less white matter damage**, according to a study on older adults in Sweden[45].

How fibre boosts our brain

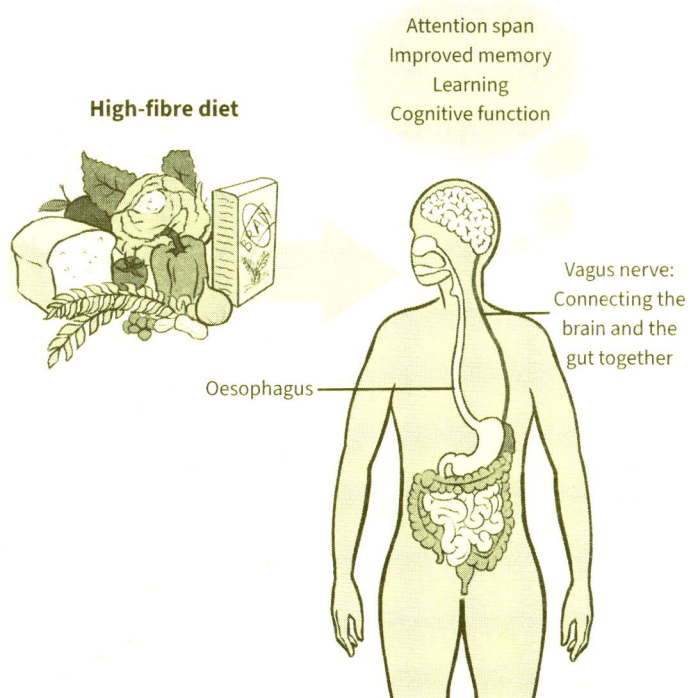

Your secret hack for looking younger

From helping your skin to glow more, to supporting the anti-ageing process, fibre is one of the best-kept beauty secrets. By boosting the amount of fibre in your diet you are supporting the health of something called the 'gut–skin axis'. We will talk about gut health in a lot more detail in the next chapter, but for now it is useful to know that the 'gut–skin axis' refers to the connection and relationship between the skin and the gut – so what you eat has a knock-on effect on the health of your digestive system, which in turn has an impact on your skin and its appearance.

How can fibre improve your skin?

It helps reduce premature wrinkles: We know that an unhealthy gut is associated with more inflammation, impaired skin barrier function, as well as something we call 'oxidative stress', which are all associated with accelerating the breakdown of collagen in our skin – a protein that promotes skin elasticity and helps us look younger. Dietary fibre, especially prebiotic fibres such as those found in flaxseed, asparagus and oats, are some of the best things to eat to support a healthier gut and in turn help to keep our skin looking more youthful. Eating a higher-fibre diet, especially one that contains resistant starch and inulin, can also lead to reduced inflammation in the body[46] – inflammation can weaken the skin barrier and contribute to wrinkle development and sagging of the skin.

It improves acne: We know from research studies that generally improving diet quality can help improve acne in some people, but much of this may be down to boosting fibre content and its effect on our gut health. One study on young adults over a six-month period showed that those who had the highest intakes of dietary fibre as well as consuming a diet with a lower glycaemic index had less severe acne breakouts, with the study demonstrating people's fibre intake being the 'strongest predictor of improved acne severity'[47,48]. Skin breakouts aren't the only complications associated with acne – many people who suffer with this skin condition may also experience skin scarring or smaller lesions as a result. In one animal study, it was seen that skin healed faster, and scar formation was accelerated in mice who were fed a high-fibre diet versus mice fed a low-fibre diet [49].

It may improve eczema, psoriasis and rosacea: Improvements in diet quality (which usually includes eating more fibre) can lead to reduced severity of some skin conditions[50]. Eating more fibre may be beneficial for those suffering with psoriasis[51], with one study showing that those who consumed significantly higher levels of fibre had lower psoriasis severity[52]. Fibre has also been noted to help with rosacea, a condition which causes flushing or redness of the face. Several studies have reported that those who suffer with rosacea may have a higher prevalence of gastrointestinal diseases and conditions like IBD, IBS or Crohn's, which can often be triggered or worsened by low-fibre intake. By including more fibre-rich foods like oats, wholegrains, pulses and vegetables, it may be possible to ease symptoms for some people and support management of this condition, which affects an estimated 5% of the global population[53].

A fibre-rich diet paired with probiotics may also work well in helping reduce the risk and severity of atopic dermatitis[54] (a type of eczema). One study following over 13,000 young Chinese adults found that those who had a high intake of fibre from their diet had lower odds of experiencing atopic dermatitis flare-ups, especially when taking a probiotic drink multiple times a week. This may be down to fibre's abilities to support and help strengthen the skin barrier, which can help to block allergens and pathogens that can cause a flare-up of the condition. There have also been several studies which show exciting advancements in treating eczema in children. One review of multiple research studies reported that baby formula supplemented with a mixture of prebiotic fibres may even prevent atopic dermatitis in infants up to two years old[55].

Fibre doesn't just benefit our skin when we eat it – it is being added to topical skincare products, too! If you suffer from acne or eczema, seeking out products that have added prebiotics like inulin or glucomannan can help to support something called the 'skin microbiome': bacteria and other microorganisms that live on our skin that help to protect it from harmful substances in our environment.

Fibre can support mental health

One of the most exciting benefits of eating a fibre-rich diet is the impact that it can have on your mental health. We are starting to learn that those who include more of it in their diet may have lower risks of anxiety as well as depression – an advancement that could be life-changing for so many. Of course, I am not suggesting that a high-fibre diet alone can cure conditions like anxiety and depression – there are many other factors involved, and everyone's circumstances are different – however, the data from recent studies is compelling. Fibre is said to be linked with mental health improvements due to its ability to positively impact gut bacteria (more on this in the next chapter), which is associated with better moods, as well as producing anti-inflammatory metabolites that can benefit the brain. These benefits that fibre has on gut bacteria can also be linked to increased production of 'happy hormones' like serotonin and dopamine, having a positive impact on how we feel.

An important note: Fibre should not be used to treat or as a cure for mental health disorders. Please ensure you also seek professional help and medical assistance if required.

MENTAL HEALTH AND FIBRE: WHAT THE DATA SAYS

- Eating more fibre is linked with a 10% lower risk of developing depression[56].
- Individuals who eat the highest amount of dietary fibre may have a lower risk of experiencing anxiety compared[57] to those who eat less[58].
- With every 5g increase in fibre you consume, you can lower your risk of developing depression by 5%[59].
- Fibre from vegetables has been shown in several studies to potentially be the most significant in lowering people's risk of depression[60].
- Eating more prebiotic fibres like inulin (found in Jerusalem artichokes and onions, for example) can help increase specific types of bacteria in our gut which may have antidepressant effects[61].

In many studies, some of the effects linking mental health and fibre may not specifically be down to fibre alone, but fibre alongside a combination of other powerful components (such as polyphenols and different vitamins, for example) that are included in people's diets. It should also be noted that those suffering with mental health disorders such as anxiety and depression may be less likely to eat a more varied diet higher in fibre, which also may have an impact on the data. Nonetheless, fibre is important and can play a big role in supporting those with mental health conditions via the gut–brain axis (see page 36).

Fibre: The list goes on

Can fibre reduce 'forever chemicals'? At the time of writing this book, there have been some small advancements showing that dietary fibre (particularly beta-glucans) may potentially play a role in reducing levels of toxic PFAs (perfluoroalkyl substances – which are nicknamed 'forever chemicals') in the body[62]. These chemicals are not broken down well, so accumulate in the body and brain, and exposure to higher levels is associated with liver damage and damage to the thyroid – not good news for our long-term health. While it is still early days and more research needs to be done, it's a glimpse into the potential power of fibre in this area.

Hormone balance: Fibre may also play a role in lowering higher levels of circulating oestrogen concentrations in the body, which could play a role in lowering breast cancer risk[63] and endometriosis[64]. Oestrogen is a hormone that ensures the correct functioning of the ovaries and uterus in women, plays a role in sustaining the strength of our bones, supports metabolism and even supports testicular function in men, too. Data has shown us that by increasing the amount of fibre you eat, you can bring down circulating oestrogen levels[65] by up to 25%[66], which is good news for those looking to support hormone balance and reproductive health if their oestrogen levels are too high.

Whole Body Benefits

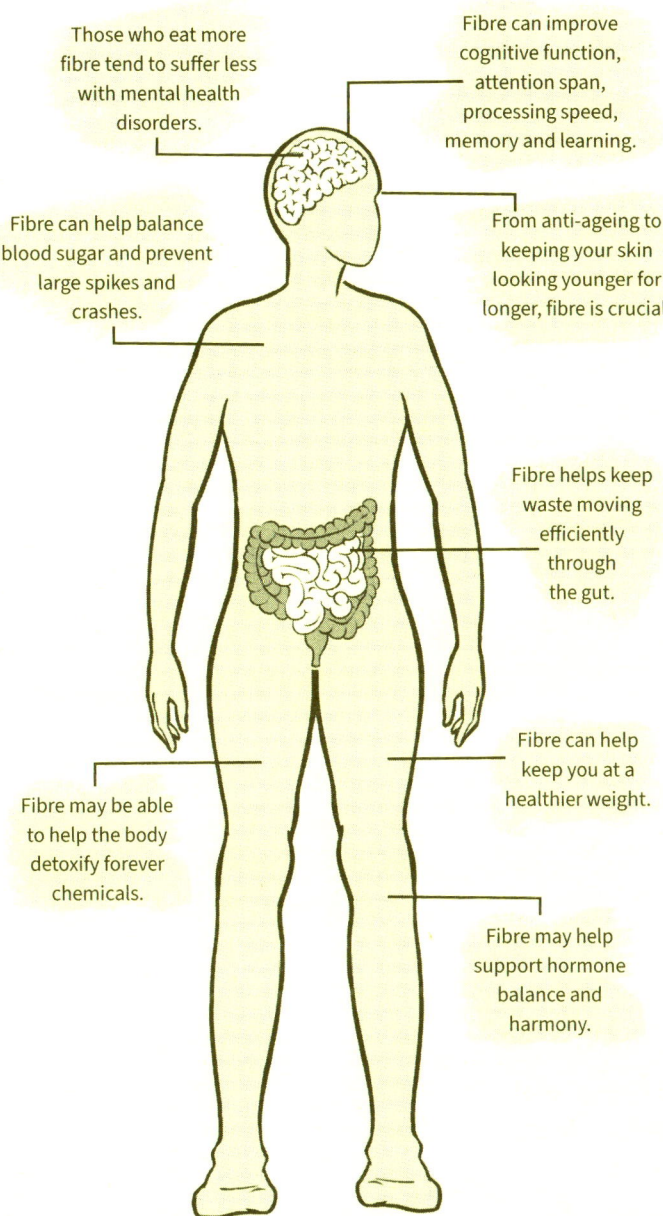

CRUNCHING THE NUMBERS (NOT JUST THE VEG) ON FIBRE TARGETS

Now that you know just how impressive fibre is, you may be wondering how much you need to be eating each day. As I touched on earlier, it is recommended in the UK for healthy adults to consume **30g daily**, with US guidelines varying by age and gender slightly – the recommendations range from 25g to 30g. The average intake in the UK currently is only around 19g according to the National Diet and Nutrition Survey (and even less in low-income households), with the US seeing a daily average intake of around only 15g a day (British Dietetic Association).

The harsh reality of current fibre intakes

- Less than 1 in 10 adults in the UK are consuming enough fibre each day.
- Over 90% of women and 97% of men in the US do not meet the recommended amounts for fibre each day[67].

The above statistics are quite shocking and help explain why many people around the globe are struggling with their health. We are seeing rates of diseases such as colon cancer on the rise, especially in young people, increased rates of people dying from preventable conditions like heart disease, and a surge in numbers of those being diagnosed with type 2 diabetes. In fact, in the UK alone, it was reported that there was an almost *40% increase* in numbers of young people being diagnosed with type 2 diabetes over a five-year period[68]. Every three seconds someone in the world develops dementia, and as an ageing population it is expected that rates of chronic conditions like cancer and arthritis will keep rising. Fibre, of course, is not the answer to *every* health issue, but it absolutely can help reduce the risk of so many of these life-threatening diseases, which we will talk more about in Chapter 4.

So, why should you be getting 30g fibre daily if you want to support better health? Well, the science shows us that those who consume a higher level of fibre from their diet have a lower risk of death from all causes, including cardiovascular diseases[69,70,71], which has been named the 'world's biggest killer' by the World Health Organization[72]. A higher fibre intake has also been shown to increase beneficial gut bacteria[73], reduce risk of colon cancer[74] and diverticular disease, support brain health as well as lower the rate of weight gain through life[75].

We know that hitting the recommended fibre intake or going slightly over this each day supports good health. But do the benefits increase the more we have? This is one of the questions I'm asked most frequently when it comes to fibre. Although research is still limited, it can be said that there is a 'dose-response relationship': this means that the more we consume, the greater the benefits – but only up to a point. Research indicates that the best protective benefits come from consuming at least 25–29g per day, so aiming for 30g (or more!) is a smart move to make sure you're getting the full effect[76]. Despite this recommendation, there are many rural populations such as the Hadza tribe – based in rural Tanzania – who consume up to 120g per day and are said to have the healthiest guts in the world, with low prevalence of biomarkers of chronic disease such as cardiovascular disease and low rates of type 2 diabetes. Much of this may also be down to their intake of less ultra-processed food and higher rates of physical activity, but the high intake of fibre may also have a huge impact on their health outcomes.

How do I know if I am getting enough?

In Part 2 of this book, I will show you how to measure your fibre intake exactly each day, and then how to fill the gap. But, there is also another easy way that you can measure if you are consuming enough fibre – just peek into the toilet bowl. Naturally, most people do not like the thought of having to look into the loo after they have gone to the bathroom, but it is one of the easiest and cheapest hacks (because it is free!) that not only could help you determine if you need more fibre, but it could also be lifesaving and help you discover signs of things like colon cancer. The Bristol Stool Chart, which can be found online, is an excellent visual guide that shows the type of poo you need to be looking for each time you go. It is also a great way to assess if your diet is healthy enough and if your fibre intake is optimal. The chart isn't just a guide for fibre intake, because there can be many other factors that influence what our poo looks like, but in a lot of cases, if you are experiencing runny 'unstructured' stools it could be an indicator that your fibre intake needs to increase. Or alternatively, if your poos are difficult to pass and resemble rabbit droppings, you may need to improve your diet quality and drink more water. A smooth, 'sausage-like' poo is ideal, and can indicate that your diet is healthy and your fibre intake is adequate. Every person is different, and it is important to remember that there may be many other factors contributing to stool type alongside fibre intake.

As well as looking into the loo, there may be other physical symptoms or signs that your fibre intake is not where it should be. Fibre helps us feel full and satisfied, so when our meals are low in it then we are more likely to feel hungry again soon after eating. If you are familiar with this feeling, then this may be your body's way of telling you to eat more higher-fibre foods. If you are also someone who experiences constipation quite regularly, this can be another common sign that you are running low on fibre. For reference, going to the bathroom anywhere from three times a day to three times a week is considered 'normal' – however, if you see unusual changes then it is a good idea to go to your doctor and get a second opinion, just to be safe. If your doctor tells you that there are no underlying issues, yet you still struggle with being a little backed up, slowly and incrementally increase your fibre over time and ensure you are also drinking enough water (see page 76). Issues with mood, sleep, feeling bloated and gassy and/or even having high cholesterol can also be signs that you could benefit with more fibre in your diet. And lastly, the feeling of 'incomplete evacuation' may be a sign that your fibre intake needs to be boosted. Have you ever gone to the bathroom but, once you have finished, felt like you hadn't properly 'emptied'? That 'incomplete' feeling may stem from many factors – a lack of fibre being one of them.

Note: If your stool changes colour drastically, there is blood in it, or you have a change in frequency or consistency, then it is a good idea to consult your doctor, just to ensure there is nothing else going on.

CHAPTER 3

Fibre and the Gut

When it comes to learning about fibre and just how important it is for us, the gut deserves its own dedicated section in this book. Our gut is *fundamental* when it comes to helping us break down fibre and processing it, as well as helping us gain the wonderful benefits from it.

When I ask people what they think their gut is, many assume that it is just the stomach – however, the gut is much more than this. It starts in our mouth and includes our oesophagus, stomach, large and small intestines, and rectum, and ends at the anus. Think of the gut as a kind of 'rollercoaster ride', where food enters at the beginning (the mouth), gets changed and broken down along the journey, all the goodness absorbed (like vitamins, minerals, energy, etc.) and then waste products exit through the other end (anus). It is estimated that around 60 tonnes of food will pass through the gut or gastrointestinal tract in an average lifetime[77] – that is the same weight as nearly nine large African elephants!

Not only this, but our gut is also involved in things like our mental health, cognitive function, how well our immune system works and even things like how fast we age, as we touched on in Chapter 2. Many of these processes are linked through something we call the **'gut–brain' axis**, which describes how these two organs are connected both physically – through something called the vagus nerve – and chemically, through things like 'neurotransmitters'. This two-way connection between the gut and brain is behind what we describe as 'gut feelings' – the butterflies we feel in our stomach when we are nervous, or even the feeling of needing to 'go' when we experience anxiety or stress. This connection can also explain why the health of our gut has a direct impact on how well our brain functions, influencing mental health, mood and focus.

And it is not just the gut and brain that are connected, but our gut and our skin, too. We know from scientific research that the skin's appearance can largely be determined by how healthy our gut is, through the 'gut–skin' axis.

You may have heard of the term 'gut health' – it seems to be everywhere right now, thanks to many new discoveries in the research world. There is no set definition for 'gut health', but many say that a 'healthy gut' means that our gut functions well, our digestion is normal, we have an absence of disease and we possess a healthy and diverse gut microbiome.

A summary

The Gut	This is the gastrointestinal tract that is responsible for digesting food and drink: the long system and pathway that food travels through, starting at the mouth and ending at the anus. It also includes the oesophagus, stomach, small and large intestines.
Gut Health	The health and wellbeing of the gut. A healthy gut is one that works optimally with an absence of disease and illness, while digesting food well.
The Gut Microbiome	The collection of things we call 'microorganisms', that live within your gut – mostly in our large intestine (more about this below).

The Gut Microbiome

The gut microbiome is one of the most fascinating areas of human health that has been discovered to date. Within our gut lives trillions of different 'microbes' (mostly bacteria) – weighing roughly 200g in total[78]. This community of microorganisms – the gut microbiome – is found mainly in your large intestine, but we do also have some residing in our small intestine, stomach[79] and other areas of the digestive tract. The gut microbiome is where a lot of the magic happens when it comes to fibre, because it is where fibre is broken down by our gut bacteria. Gut bacteria are the superheroes of fibre digestion, because as humans we cannot digest it on our own: we rely 100% on our gut bacteria to do this job. Gut bacteria contain many different enzymes (which humans do not possess) that can ferment fibre that we eat in our food and in turn produce health-boosting 'metabolites' for us. This is why I always say that 'fibre isn't food for us, it's food for our gut bugs'.

It has been shown that if you are someone who smokes, has a low-fibre diet, drinks alcohol regularly, lacks sufficient sleep and/or consumes too much ultra-processed food, this can negatively impact how healthy your gut microbiome is, potentially leading to something called 'gut dysbiosis'. Gut dysbiosis is an imbalance between good and bad bacteria, which can cause problems for your immune system, leaving you more susceptible to infectious diseases[80]. We also know that geographic location may impact your gut microbiome – those living in rural locations may possess a wider variety of good bacteria as part of their gut microbiome, compared to those living in more urban settings like cities. However, more research needs to be done in this area and factors such as quality of life may also have an impact on results seen in studies so far.

IT STARTS AT BIRTH

Your method of birth delivery can also have an impact on your gut microbiome, especially in infancy[81] but also potentially later in life. Infants who are born vaginally tend to possess different gut bacteria than those born via C-section. Studies are still investigating the impact this may have on our health later in life.

Gut bacteria metabolites

When gut bacteria digest and ferment the soluble fibre we eat, they produce an array of different health-boosting compounds and nutrients for our bodies. I describe it as a mutually beneficial agreement – we provide a nice warm home (inside our gut) for them, we feed them regularly (when we eat fibre), and in turn they pay us rent (by providing us with various nutrients and metabolites that can support our health). The following nutrients and metabolites are some of the most important created in this process:

B vitamins
Our intake of healthy food is the main source of vitamins and minerals, but our gut bugs can also act as a 'vitamin factory', helping top up the levels of vitamin K as well as most of the B vitamins. In fact, it has been discovered that your gut bacteria can even produce up to 30% of your daily recommended intakes of vitamins B6, B9 and B12[82]! Our gut bacteria will keep most of the vitamins they synthesize, using them to support their own growth and overall health, but the remainder is then used by us to support processes including immune function, energy production, the nervous system (B vitamins) as well as playing a role in blood clotting and bone health (vitamin K).

Neurotransmitters
Gut bacteria also produce a range of super-cool molecules called 'neurotransmitters'. Neurotransmitters are chemical signals which act like little messengers, carrying information from one nerve cell to the next. Some of the more well-known neurotransmitters include dopamine (the 'reward' neurotransmitter) and serotonin (usually called the 'happy hormone'), which are made in the gut but also by the brain. Serotonin and dopamine made in the brain

directly affect our mood and behaviour, but when these neurotransmitters are produced in the gut by our gut bacteria, they can play a slightly different role. Down there, their main aim is to help keep your digestion running smoothly by supporting muscle contractions, aiding in the release of digestive fluids, and help to maintain the gut's protective barrier. But your gut bacteria don't just stop at dopamine and serotonin – they are known to produce over 30 other neurotransmitters[83], which includes GABA (which helps regulate gut activity and promote 'calmness') and 'norepinephrine' – also known as noradrenaline – which plays a role in immune function as well as supporting digestion.

Short-chain fatty acids

We now know that we cannot digest fibre ourselves – we need our gut bacteria to munch on it and help to ferment it. As a result of this process, we get powerful compounds called short-chain fatty acids – 'SCFAs' for short. If you asked me to name some of my favourite gut health topics, SCFAs would be right at the top of that list because, as you will see, they are just so impressive.

Fibre fuels your gut bacteria to produce health-boosting SCFAs

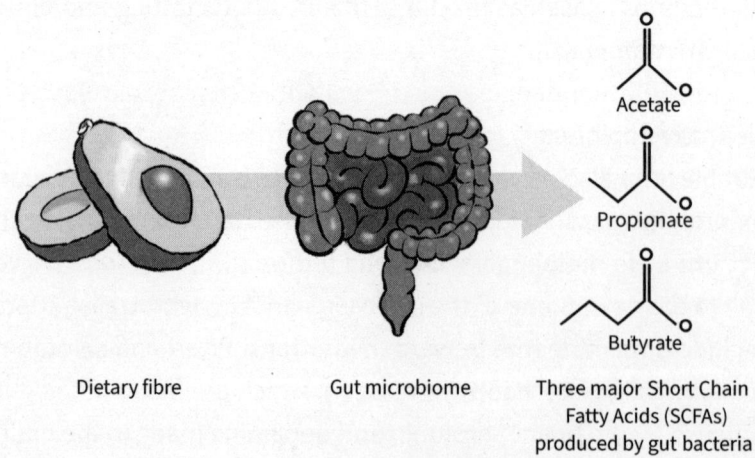

Dietary fibre   Gut microbiome   Three major Short Chain Fatty Acids (SCFAs) produced by gut bacteria

How can SCFAs support our health?

1. They're our immune system besties

SCFAs are one of the key players when it comes to our body's immune function. Not only can they help to calm down inflammation when it is not needed, but they promote inflammatory responses[84] when it is – for example, when we get an infection. Some SCFAs, like butyrate, can also play a role in strengthening the gut barrier[85] – helping to block disease-causing organisms trying to get through. Their ability to support the gut barrier also helps prevent 'leaky gut'. Leaky gut is exactly what it says on the tin – it occurs when your gut barrier becomes more permeable, leaking tiny harmful molecules and waste products out of the gut and into the bloodstream[86]. This isn't great news for our health and may be associated with conditions such as autism[87] or dementia[88].

SCFAS AND IBD

SCFAs are showing promising results in treatment for Inflammatory Bowel Disease (IBD)[89], which includes conditions like Crohn's and Ulcerative Colitis. These conditions involve chronic gut inflammation that can lead to pain, nutritional deficiencies, ulcers and an increased risk of developing colon cancer. People with IBD may have altered levels of SCFAs, which can lead to more inflammation and leaky gut. Increasing dietary fibre can boost SCFA production, helping to reduce inflammation and supporting healing in the gut[90]. Research in this area is ongoing, but findings are encouraging. If you have IBD, consult your doctor before making dietary changes.

2. They are the main energy source for the colon

When our fibre-fuelled gut bugs produce different SCFAs, our colon cells then use these as their primary energy source[91]. More specifically, these colon cells get between 60 and 70% of their energy from SCFAs like butyrate. Without them, digestion would be disturbed and we could see long-term negative impacts on our health.

3. They help you feel full and satisfied

We know that fibre can help us to feel fuller for longer, as it can bulk up stools and slow down digestion, but SCFAs such as propionate can also be a great tool when it comes to weight management. Not only do SCFAs help to promote satiety (feeling full), but they can also stimulate the release of hormones GLP-1[92] (commonly used in weight-loss medications like Ozempic) as well as 'PYY'[93] – a hormone involved in appetite regulation and supporting a healthy body weight.

4. They support brain function

SCFAs can influence how gut bacteria communicate with the brain and may impact brain function. They can also reduce neuroinflammation[94] (inflammation in the brain), which has been linked to conditions such as Alzheimer's and Parkinson's disease[95]. In addition, SCFAs also have the power to potentially boost the production of brain-building cells[96], which is good news if you are looking to maintain mental sharpness as you age.

5. They are stress-busting

Because SCFAs can influence the brain, they can also help contribute to improved mental wellbeing, leading to you potentially feeling less stressed when your gut bacteria are making enough[97]. In one animal study, SCFAs were given to mice, and this reduced their stress hormone response[98]. In another study on humans, it was seen that SCFAs administered to the large intestine reduced the body's release of cortisol in response to stressful social situations[99].

SCFAS CAN IMPROVE NUTRIENT ABSORPTION

Some short-chain fatty acids may help increase absorption of minerals like calcium and magnesium[100,101], which can be helpful, especially since so many of us run low in these two minerals. This may be because SCFAs have the potential to lower the pH of the gut, making it more acidic and potentially improving mineral solubility and absorption. Scientists also suggest that SCFAs can play a role in increasing the surface area of your gut lining, allowing for greater absorption of these health-boosting minerals[102].

The amount of SCFAs being produced depends on your age, activity level, fibre intake, diet quality, as well as presence or lack of certain bacterial 'species' in your gut. Species such as some that are part of the Bifidobacterium, Bacteroides *and* Clostridium *groups (or genera) tend to have powerful SCFA-producing abilities. To boost the presence of these in your gut, eat more fruit like blueberries and prunes, vegetables like leeks, beans and onions, wholegrains like oats, and fermented foods like sauerkraut and kimchi[103].*

What happens to our gut when we do not consume enough fibre?

As we now know, fibre is fundamental to the health of our gut bacteria. But what happens if we do not get enough of it? For example, if we are on a very low carbohydrate diet, or we are eating a diet very high in ultra-processed foods? Well, this can start to starve our gut bugs, leaving them so ravenous that they begin to munch away at the mucous lining of our intestines[104]. This lining protects our gut, supports immune function and helps to keep waste moving along the digestive system so that it doesn't get 'stuck'. This mucous lining is the next best source of nutrition, containing a rich source of 'glycoproteins' – molecules that are made up of protein that also have carbohydrate chains attached to them. The gut mucous layer then becomes thinner, weaker and inflamed and can contribute to leaky gut, inflammatory conditions like diverticulitis and ulcerative colitis, as well as weakening our immune system.

A low-fibre intake reduces the diversity of beneficial gut bacteria and can weaken them, too. This is bad news for our health. The imbalance increases the risk of conditions such as cardiovascular disease, obesity, type 2 diabetes and mental health disorders like depression and anxiety (more on this in Chapter 4). Much of this is linked to reduced production of health-boosting SCFAs by our gut bacteria. And the negative effect on our gut microbiome may not be limited to just our own bodies – it could potentially affect our offspring, too. In one animal study, mice fed a low-fibre diet showed a depletion in beneficial gut bacteria that lasted for up to four generations of offspring[105].

As discussed in Chapter 2, fibre plays a key role in keeping things moving through the gut. Without adequate fibre, your gut becomes slow, sluggish and stagnant. Food waste moves through the digestive system more slowly, leading to excess gas and allows toxic waste to remain in your gut for longer – not great news when it comes to reducing inflammation in your body or lowering your risk of conditions like colon cancer.

Self experiment
While writing this book, I was interested in investigating the impact of a low-fibre diet on my gut, so I decided to conduct my own experiment: for three weeks, I consumed a low-fibre diet (no more than 15g a day), followed by three weeks of a high-fibre diet (at least 30g daily).

Not only were there changes in my gut microbiome, but I also felt *profoundly* different when doing the two different diets. When my consumption of fibre was low, I felt hungrier between meals, tended to snack more often, had lower moods, struggled with sleep and felt less energized. For someone who is used to consuming a high-fibre diet, I also found it quite an adjustment and it was tricky to find low-fibre healthy foods, so I'd find myself resorting to unhealthier options such as white bread and white pasta just to ensure I wasn't consuming more than 15g in the entire day. I couldn't eat much fruit or veg, so was limited to mostly high-protein, high-fat, highly-processed carbohydrates that left my gut struggling and made me feel bloated and lethargic, too. And this lower-fibre regime wasn't just affecting how I felt. My gut microbiome test results* indicated a lower level of beneficial bacterial species present in my gut, such as *Faecalibacterium prausnitzii*, *Bifidobacterium longum* and *Coprococcus eutactus*, as well as a reduced presence of beneficial strains of *E. coli* and *Lactobacillus* (compared to the average person's sample). Levels of pathogenic bacteria were still low, however – I expect three weeks may have been too short a time to have any significant effect. It would be interesting to repeat this experiment for longer to see if there are any changes in this area.

The high-fibre three weeks which followed changed things dramatically. Not only were my meals more vibrant, colourful and healthier, but I found that I snacked less between meals due to the higher-fibre meals keeping me feeling fuller for longer. My mood improved, I was sleeping better and my menstrual phase seemed like less of a drag. My gut microbiome test results showed improvements: in just three weeks, there was a small increase in the amount of beneficial gut bacteria present in my low-fibre diet stool sample. I saw increases in *Faecalibacterium prausnitzii* and *Bifidobacterium longum*, a reduced 'risk' score for developing Crohn's as well as ulcerative colitis, and an increase in my gut microbiome diversity score.

It is important to note that this was just a simple experiment conducted by myself at home, but nevertheless, the results are quite impressive. If we can see changes in our gut microbiome after just three weeks of eating better, imagine how much impact this could have on our health if we adopted a high-fibre diet long term?

Note: While a gut microbiome test kit proved useful in this context, I do not recommend them for routine or everyday purposes. They are expensive and are not necessary for the average person. Instead, aim to boost your diet with high-fibre foods, consume more probiotic-rich foods like yoghurt, sauerkraut and other fermented foods, reduce stress, and follow the other recommendations in this book to see improvements in your gut microbiome.

CHAPTER 4

Fibre is Key to Preventing Disease

It is estimated, at the time of writing, that the cost of chronic disease across the globe is to reach *$47 trillion* in the next five years. Despite such great advancements being made in science and medicine, the worsening quality of our diets remains one of the leading drivers behind rising rates, as well as their mounting economic burden.

Fibre is often overlooked as a tool for disease prevention because people are not aware of just how powerful it can be. What if I told you that there is a mountain of evidence proving that fibre supports our body's health so we can defend ourselves against many diseases? It does this through a variety of mechanisms, including helping us to keep ourselves at a healthy weight, supporting more balanced blood sugar levels, strengthening our gut barrier and reducing inflammation – mainly via something called the 'gut–immune' axis.

What is the Gut–Immune Axis?

'All disease begins in the gut'
HIPPOCRATES

Just like the gut–brain and the gut–skin axis, we also have something called the 'gut–immune' axis – the connection between our gut microbiome and our immune system. It plays a big role in helping us defend ourselves against different diseases and infections. A staggering **70–80% of our immune system cells are housed in our gut,** and our gut bacteria and the short-chain fatty acids they produce act like little warriors, helping to protect these immune cells by safeguarding the intestinal barrier and helping to defend against pathogens (harmful microorganisms) by blocking their ability to multiply and cause damage to our health.

Gut bacteria can also communicate with, train and educate some of these immune system cells, helping them distinguish between harmful pathogens and friendly microbes, as well as influencing how efficiently they react to threats. Keeping gut bacteria strong and healthy by consuming enough fibre each day for them to feed on and ferment powers them up so that they can do their job correctly. So, how can these warriors future-proof us from diseases?

Colon cancer

Colon cancer is currently the third most common cancer in the world, according to the World Health Organization, and is associated with a high risk of death. Shockingly, cases of colon cancer in young people have almost *doubled* since 1990[106]. It has been said that if these trends continue, we may see around 50% of people experiencing at least one colorectal tumour (with roughly a 10% chance of it then turning cancerous) by the time they reach 70[107]. Many factors, such as the increase in ultra-processed foods consumption, alcohol consumption and other lifestyle factors that compromise our health, may have an effect on cancer development, however, many experts claim that low fibre intake may contribute to it, too.

But, there is good news: every 10g of fibre we eat is associated with a 10% lower risk of colon cancer, particularly with the fibre found in cereals and wholegrains[108]. How does fibre help in reducing colon cancer risk? Firstly, it can help shorten the time that waste products sit in our intestines, so potential cancer-causing substances (the result of digestion of certain foods) have less time to interact with your gut wall and cause damage. Secondly, as we covered in the last chapter, many of our wonderful gut bacteria produce SCFAs for us when we eat fibre. These SCFAs support colon health and reduce inflammation, and some (such as acetate, propionate and butyrate) may even have tumour-suppressing properties, too[109,110]. Low levels of some SCFAs like butyrate, acetate and propionate have been associated with a higher risk of colon cancer in some studies[111,112,113], so ensuring your fibre intake is optimal is important.

The fibre we eat may play a role in slowing down the growth of certain colon cancer cells by 'binding up' bile acids. Bile acids are useful fluids made by your liver that help your body break down and digest fats that we eat. Think of the last meal you ate that contained a fat source like cheese, eggs or even pizza – your liver was pumping out bile acids to help them break down properly in your digestive system. While these acids are important, if too many of them are present in the colon or are made by our gut bacteria (called secondary bile acids), without fibre helping to excrete them effectively, they can pose a risk and boost the growth of colon cancer cells[114,115].

FIBRE IN COLON CANCER TREATMENT

Fibre can also be useful in assisting the treatment of colon cancer. The structure of certain types, such as lignin and pectin, enables them to carry life-saving drugs through most of the gut without being broken down, so they only break down in the colon and therefore release the drugs directly at tumour sites while minimizing damage to any surrounding healthy cells[116,117]. Smart, right?

Alzheimer's disease

Growing up with a family member who suffered from Alzheimer's disease, I have seen the negative impact it can have not only on an individual's quality of life, but how extremely difficult it can be for those around them. It is estimated that **up to 35% of Alzheimer's cases can be prevented**[118] through lifestyle factors, which include diet quality, and more specifically, scientists have drawn associations between fibre intake and Alzheimer's risk.

It has been found that the more fibre people tend to eat, the lower their risk of developing Alzheimer's, as well as other forms of dementia, later in life[119]. This may be due to fibre's ability to reduce inflammation and improve cognitive function via the gut–brain axis, as well as its role in managing other symptoms that may put someone at increased risk of developing the disease, such as high blood pressure or obesity. In some animal studies, soluble fibre in particular has been shown to boost beneficial gut bacteria and SCFAs, which may play a role in reducing Alzheimer's risk[120].

Cardiovascular diseases (CVD)

If you are a little younger, you might look at this section and be tempted to skip it simply because 'cardiovascular disease' can seem like the type of thing that only affects older people. However, cardiovascular diseases develop over a long period of time and the habits you build in your younger years play a big role.

BIGGEST KILLER

CVD is a term we use for all the conditions that affect your heart and blood vessels – also including heart disease and stroke – which can be life-threatening. In fact, CVDs are the **leading cause of death** in the USA[121], and account for nearly **half of all deaths** in Europe[122].

The power of fibre for your heart

If you want to work on reducing your risk of developing cardiovascular diseases, research shows that boosting your fibre intake can be one of the best places to start. In one meta-analysis looking at data from over 1.4 million people, it was found that those who consumed around 29g of fibre per day had a **23% lower risk of dying from cardiovascular diseases, and a 24% lower risk of death by heart disease** (a type of cardiovascular disease). Interestingly, this study also found that people who ate more fibre from cereals (things like oats, brown rice and wholegrains) had a lower risk of developing cardiovascular disease compared to those who got their fibre from other sources[123].

To support your heart through the power of fibre, aim to get at least one portion of wholegrains into your diet every single day. This could look like switching the coffee and breakfast muffin you usually grab on the go for a quick and easy porridge pot, adding a serving of brown rice alongside the mixed salad and chicken breast you are having for lunch, or mixing some quinoa into beef patties or veggie burgers you make at home for dinner!

In 2015, a review of several large studies was carried out by the UK's Scientific Advisory Committee on Nutrition (SACN), and it was found that for every 7g increase in fibre participants consumed, there was a 9% reduction in their risk of developing cardiovascular disease.

Researchers have also found that eating a higher-fibre diet may also give those who have survived a heart attack a greater chance of living for longer. In a review of data from over 4,000 men and women, it was found that those who ate the most amount of fibre had a 25% lower risk of death in the nine years after their heart attack[124]. But how exactly does fibre work its magic and help us reduce our risk of these diseases? Well firstly, fibre (particularly soluble fibre) can act as a sort of 'sponge', soaking up some of the bad cholesterol, helping to lower it. Having high cholesterol is one of the biggest risk factors for developing cardiovascular diseases, because the build-up of it restricts blood flow and increases the risk of heart attack and stroke.

Fibre also helps by lowering blood pressure. High blood pressure affects over 1.3 billion people globally and is one of the major risk factors for developing CVDs. In one study of 1.25 million people, it was discovered that those who had high blood pressure at the age of 30 had a 63% chance of developing cardiovascular disease at some point in their life. In another review of multiple studies, it was found that those who adopted a higher-fibre diet saw significant changes in their blood pressure, independent of medications[125]. Hearing stats like this really makes me want to shout from the rooftops about how adding more fibre to our diets could help so many people. The array of evidence grows by the day, as does the number of cases of killer diseases like diabetes, stroke and obesity, why aren't healthcare organisations giving diet quality higher priority?

Fibre's cardiovascular-supporting powers don't stop there. One of the factors that can increase your risk of developing cardiovascular diseases is being overweight or obese, and because fibre can regulate our appetite and help us manage our weight (as we discussed in Chapter 2), it may be a useful tool in CVD prevention long term.

Breast cancer

Breast cancer is the most common cancer to be diagnosed for women in the world[126], with almost 57,000 new cases being recorded on average in the UK per year according to Cancer Research UK, and over 315,000 being estimated to be diagnosed in the US in 2025. These are scary figures, but the good news is that almost a quarter of these cases may be preventable[127] by changing up our lifestyle, and you guessed it – boosting our fibre content! Similar to how it can help with preventing colon cancer, fibre can help our gut bugs produce SCFAs which help to clear up some inflammation in the body, while also helping to stop or slow down cancer stem cells from multiplying as they can have anti-tumor effects[128].

THE LOWDOWN ON BREAST CANCER AND FIBRE

- High fibre consumption is associated with a decreased risk of breast cancer.
- According to one meta-analysis (a study of lots of different studies pooled together), there is an 11% decreased risk of developing breast cancer in people with the highest intake of fibre[129].
- In the same study as above, it was discovered that there was a 7% decreased risk of people getting breast cancer for every 10g increment of fibre they added to their diet.
- Not only can fibre potentially reduce your risk of developing breast cancer, but it has been found that eating a high-fibre diet can actually prolong your lifespan after being diagnosed with the disease, too[130].
- Fibre from plant foods we eat can also help to bind to excess oestrogen in the gut, preventing it from being reabsorbed back into the bloodstream[131]. Excess oestrogen is linked to an increase in breast cancer risk, so fibre can play a role in reducing it.

How can I easily add 10g of extra fibre to my diet? A breakfast of 2 slices of rye bread toast and 1 large banana adds up to over 10g fibre per day. Or how about switching your usual lower-fibre lunch for a delicious baked potato with beans and a side of coleslaw to hit 10g fibre by the afternoon?

Irritable Bowel Disease (IBD)

If you suffer with IBD, the topic of increasing your fibre intake can be a little tricky. You may feel like when you boost your fibre, it flares up your condition even more. There is evidence for this to be true, and therefore it is recommended that increasing your fibre intake too much (especially from insoluble fibre sources) should be avoided during flare-ups, fistulas or strictures. Fibre can seem a little like a double-edged sword for those with Crohn's or Ulcerative Colitis (the two different types of IBD) due to both its benefits and the symptoms that may come as a result of consuming more of it.

What we do know from studies is that the **type** of fibre can make a difference. One showed that beta-glucans (a type of fibre outlined in Chapter 1) found in foods like artichokes and chicory root can be a little more harsh on the lining of the gut for those with IBD[132] during a flare-up and contribute to more inflammation. Lower-fibre sources that are easier to digest can be a good alternative during this time, such as cooked and peeled vegetables like carrots and parsnips, or soft fruits such as melon, ripe bananas and avocados. If in doubt, speak to your dietitian.

It has been discovered that a diet high in fruit-derived fibre can be useful for those suffering with Crohn's (reducing risk by 73–80%), whereas for ulcerative colitis, vegetables appeared more protective in reducing risk[133].

We also know that those who suffer with IBD usually have a gut microbiome that is less diverse and contains fewer beneficial types of gut bacteria compared to healthy individuals. This is where a chicken-and-egg scenario comes into play: does the low intake of fibre commonly seen in those with IBD[134] contribute to the lack of good gut bacteria in the first place, or did their gut health decline because their IBD made it harder to eat a wide variety of healthy, fibrous plants due to their symptoms? Numerous studies are investigating this question, but what we do know is that each individual is different and that many other factors need to be considered in the development of this condition.

Boosting fibre intake isn't all bad news for IBD sufferers, though. During flare-ups, it is indeed recommended for individuals to stick to a lower-fibre diet, but once symptoms improve, it is advised to gradually reintroduce more fibre-containing foods where possible due to their protective effects and support for gut health. Because fibre can play a role in maintaining the health of the gut lining, it may also reduce the frequency and severity of future flare-ups, as well as contributing to boosting SCFAs, which have anti-inflammatory effects.

The bottom line when it comes to fibre intake, if you suffer from IBD, is this: everyone is different and it is important to get advice from your doctor or specialist. Work out which types of fibre and foods you tolerate best, and this can make it easier to ensure you are getting what you need to support your gut.

Type 2 Diabetes

As we touched on in Chapter 2, Type 2 diabetes is a condition where the body does not make enough of a hormone called insulin – or, if it does make it, the body cannot use it properly. As a result, sugar builds up in the bloodstream instead of being carried into the cells to be used as fuel for our body. This can lead to extreme tiredness and thirst, or even more serious long-term health issues such as damage to eyesight, the kidneys, and even heart disease. Studies indicate that boosting fibre alone may not help to prevent this condition, but it can help with management by supporting blood sugar control, aiding weight management, improving overall quality of life and reducing complications associated with the disease. Additionally, increasing fibre intake to around 35g per day is linked with a 10–48% reduced risk of premature death in people with diabetes[135]. Studies have also shown that for every 7g increase in fibre you eat, you have a 6% lower risk of developing diabetes (SACN 2015).

Adding 7g of fibre to your diet per day could be simpler than you think: try 150g of baked beans, 2 slices of thick wholemeal toast, or one portion of cooked lentils (90g).

Can fibre also help us to manage infectious diseases?

Because of fibre's ability to alter the gut microbiome while strengthening the gut barrier to protect us from harmful pathogens, it is known to play a role in helping prevent some infectious diseases. Fibre may also help reduce complications of infections by lowering inflammation, decreasing the risk of diarrhoea, and reducing the risk of hyperglycaemia. In one systematic review of 12 studies, it was found that eating more fibre was an effective way of reducing complications of viral infections in intensive care patients. Fibre also helped lower the death rate from viral infections because of its ability to influence inflammation in the body[136].

CHAPTER 5

Why Are We Ghosting the Good Stuff?

As we have seen throughout this book, our fibre intake is *far* below what it needs to be. But when something is so good for us, why don't we prioritize it more in our diet? You may be answering that question already in your own head and saying something like; 'well, it's because we didn't *know* these things!' – which brings me onto my first point:

I truly believe that if people were told more about how much fibre could help their health – reducing the risk of developing serious diseases, helping their skin glow and even extending their life – they would be on it like a rocket. But that's the problem: public health education around fibre and just how beneficial it is remains completely lacking. The health and nutrition advice we are given in school is limited to just a few mentions here and there about 'five a day'. In gyms, hospitals and offices, you might see a few posters in the cafeteria about having a balanced plate – not much, however, about fibre. The issue is that most dietary guidelines globally emphasize foods rather than specific nutrients like fibre, and they often fail to give us easy-to-understand examples of how the everyday person can incorporate it into their diet.

THE FIBRE KNOWLEDGE GAP

- Only around 7% of people in the UK are aware that they should be consuming 30g of fibre each day[137].
- In one survey, only 1 in 3 people knew that the recommended daily amount of fibre for adults was 30g, and nearly three-quarters were unaware if they met the recommended intake (Food & Drink Federation, 2025).
- Only a quarter of people know that a high-fibre diet can reduce your risk of type 2 diabetes, and over 10% of people didn't know what any of the benefits of fibre were (Food & Drink Federation, 2025).
- One UK survey by Kellogg's showed that 92% of people were not aware of how much fibre they needed to be eating daily[138], while another small study done on UK participants demonstrated that knowledge around fibre's benefits outside of digestive health was very limited[139].
- New research states that nearly two-thirds of UK adults are more likely to choose foods labelled as 'a source of fibre' or 'high in fibre'. However, around one in seven of those surveyed feel they do not have enough knowledge or guidance on how to identify foods that are high in fibre[140].

This lack of awareness around our favourite F-word is also partly down to just how 'unsexy' fibre is in the eyes of the general public. When you think of fibre, your brain may automatically go to thoughts of constipation prevention and prune juice – but, as we have seen throughout this book, fibre is *much* more than that and has been given a bit of a bad rap. We don't really talk about it as a nutrient, especially in the UK, where discussions of anything poo-related are still a little taboo.

My hopes for all the readers of this book, fully committed members of the Fibre Fix gang, is to help spread the word on just how amazing fibre is and to encourage more conversations about it. So, my task for you after finishing this chapter is to try to spark up a few fibre-focused conversations and tell your friends or family about three benefits of it from Chapter 2. When more people start talking about fibre, we can help boost how much we eat as a population over time. But what other factors might be causing people to ghost the good stuff?

Is eating more fibre too expensive?

Achieving 30g of fibre a day in today's world may also prove a little tricky for many people due to the rising costs of healthier foods like wholegrains and fruit and veg. According to the NDNS in the UK, only 17% of adults met the 5-a-day recommendation.

It frightens me as a nutritionist seeing that a cheeseburger meal from McDonald's can be cheaper than a basket full of fresh fruit, vegetables and wholegrains in the supermarket – no wonder so many of us are struggling to eat well and getting enough fibre in. We also know from the UK's 2025 Broken Plate Report that the most deprived fifth of the population in the UK would have to spend 45% of their disposable income on food to keep up with healthy eating guidelines, which includes hitting their fibre goals. That being said, there are some simple ways to keep your fibre intake high and eat more healthy foods without having to break the bank.

How to keep costs down when boosting fibre intake

There are plenty of ways to stay on budget while still eating a healthy balanced diet and also hitting your golden '30' each day, using my top tips below.

- **Buy frozen fruit and vegetables.** Most produce is picked at peak ripeness and immediately frozen, they often retain more nutrients than fresh produce that's been sitting on store shelves, and then in your cupboards, for days before being eaten. You tend to also get more for your money and because they can be stored in your freezer for much longer, it leads to less food waste, too!

- **Opt for tinned and dried foods.** With the rising cost of fresh produce, stocking up on tinned or dried foods such as beans, pulses or vegetables can be a great option. Try adding dried mushrooms into soups or stews, pouring tinned lentils into a curry or salad, or adding tinned peas to your roast dinner. In the last section of this book, you will find examples of how to use tinned and dried foods in recipes to help you hit 30g of fibre.

- **Eat fewer animal foods.** Have you noticed how much more expensive your shopping cart is when you buy more animal-based foods like meat, fish and dairy? Although these are all valuable sources of protein and micronutrients, they can be expensive. Eating a more plant-based diet with fewer animal foods can be a lot cheaper, and it will be probably contain way more fibre, too. In a review of over 43 different research studies, it was seen that those who ate a vegan diet had the highest intakes of fibre (around 44g per day), vegetarians got on average 28g, and meat-eaters showed lower intakes – only around 21g fibre per day on average.[141] Simple shifts like doing one meat-free day a week such as a 'meat-free Monday' can be great ways to boost fibre intake while also reducing food costs.

- **Buy seasonal.** Buying more seasonal fruit and vegetables can help lower the price of your food shop. For example, high-fibre berries like blackberries are more readily available and cheaper between late summer and mid autumn (I like to pick them myself or buy them in batches, wash them and store them in the freezer so that I can enjoy them out of season for a fraction of the cost). The same can be applied to fruits like strawberries (late spring and through the summer), rhubarb (early spring to late summer) and cherries (mid summer to end summer).

- **Skip organic.** Although there can be benefits to buying organic foods, it is not a necessity for good health and to hit your fibre intake. Washing your fruit and vegetables well and using bicarbonate of soda (see page 102) is sufficient. But if you find that organic food alternatives fit your budget, then you can keep it included in your shopping list!

- **Plan ahead.** When life gets busy, meal planning might feel like the last thing you want to do. But carving out just 5–10 minutes at the end of your week to plan can save you a lot of time, money and help you ensure you are smashing through your fibre goals for the week ahead. Proper planning can also make you less likely to impulse-buy or buy things you do not need (how many times have you thrown mouldy salad bags or rotten veggies from the back of the fridge in the bin?), while also reducing food waste. Get a whiteboard in your kitchen and jot down the meals for the week and the ingredients needed, and see my notes on page 122 on how to meal-prep and keep an eye on the diversity of foods.

UPFs have taken over

As ultra-processed foods (UPFs) take over our plates, fibre is slowly disappearing from our diets. UPFs are defined by NOVA (a food classification system) as foods that 'contain formulations of ingredients, mostly of exclusive industrial use, typically created by a series of industrial techniques and processes'. This is basically a fancy way of describing foods that may contain different additives, stabilizers or emulsifiers – such as ready meals, chicken nuggets, packaged sandwiches and packaged cakes and biscuits – that aren't ideal in large amounts. At the time of writing, UPFs make up around 57% of our diet in the UK and almost 58% in the US[142], making it harder than ever for us to hit our fibre intake. Typically, much of the fibre is removed from these UPF foods for ease of processing and texture, and replaced with excess fat, processed sugar or salt. This also makes them easier to eat in larger quantities, which isn't great news for our health.

One study in Switzerland of over 2,000 people examined the relationship between UPF consumption and fibre intake. They found that the more ultra-processed foods people consumed, the less fibre they got each day[143].

Not only do these ultra-processed foods taste good, but they can also be highly addictive. Regular consumption can trigger a dopamine response in the brain. This feel-good sensation doesn't last very long, but it can lead to a cycle of increased consumption over time, especially as we become more receptive to these foods and require larger quantities in order to get the same response. Chronically high intakes of UPFs have been associated with issues in the brain's dopamine system, where signals may become weaker, imbalanced, or less responsive[144].

UPFS IN OUR DIET

- Avoiding UPFs is proving harder than ever, especially when it comes to our weekly food shop. One study done by Northeastern University demonstrated that around 73% of the United States food supply is ultra-processed[145], with more than 50% being ultra-processed in the UK[146].
- One study from Brazil[147] in 2019 demonstrated that an average Brazilian would be exposed to 49,932 UPF television adverts in their lifetime. While television adverts in different parts of the world may differ depending on advertising standards, it may help explain why avoiding these foods may be so hard in some regions.

Protein Obsessed, Fibre Depressed

For the last decade or so, the spotlight has been off fibre and on something else: protein. When we think of getting healthy, eating better and getting fit, protein seems to be at the top of our list of priorities – but why? Protein is an important macronutrient that we need for growth and repair of tissues like muscle, but are we really so deficient in it that every other food in the supermarkets nowadays needs to have a 'high protein' label? A recent survey by Ocado showed that interest in high-protein foods is booming – with online searches increasing by 105% in the last year alone.

Despite what the supplement industry might suggest, most people in the west are not deficient in protein – in fact, far from it. In the UK, the average person is not only meeting their protein requirement, but actually exceeds the daily recommended intake, according to the British Nutrition Foundation. We are currently living through a **fibre deficiency crisis**, not a protein deficiency crisis. As we discussed in the last chapter, this low fibre intake is leading to more health issues, including increased rates of colon cancer in young people.

I still encourage you to eat enough protein each day (between 0.75g–1.2g protein per day per kg of body weight, depending on your activity level – see page 82 on protein requirements), as it is an important building block of all our cells, helps us feel fuller for longer, supports good skin health and much more. But, instead of obsessing over protein, shift your focus more onto tracking and prioritizing your fibre intake. Trust me, your gut will thank you for it.

The majority of our fibre intake comes from low-fibre sources

The most recent National Diet and Nutrition Survey shows that for adults in the UK aged 19–64, around 45% of their fibre intake comes from cereals and cereal products – and for children aged 11–18, it is around 50%. However, the foods people tend to choose within this category are usually lower in fibre, such as refined white bread, white pasta, and items like buns, cakes and pastries.

If we were to make simple switches to wholegrain sources, provide more education on their health impacts for the wider public, and make them more accessible, it could lead to dramatic improvements in daily fibre intake. And as you'll see in Part 2, boosting our fibre intake can be both easy and cost-effective. Small changes – like buying frozen, tinned or dried fruit and vegetables, switching to a wholemeal loaf of the same bread, or purchasing dried grains and pulses like lentils and brown rice – can ensure your weekly shop doesn't cost more than usual.

Fibre fear: meaty misinformation

We live in an era where much of what we learn on any subject comes through social media and the internet. Unfortunately, this isn't always a good thing, because false information – especially around fibre – can spread like wildfire and negatively impact people's choices. In a recent study by calorie-tracking app MyFitnessPal, it was found that only 2.1% of health and nutrition advice on TikTok was accurate. *Two point one per cent!*

When it comes to fibre, the misinformation on social media is particularly concerning from a nutritionist's perspective. With the rise in popularity of diets like carnivore and low-carb, we are seeing a lot of fear-mongering about fibre and claims that we should even *avoid* it. As you have learnt throughout this book, that approach is the exact opposite of what truly supports our long-term health. But when extreme diet communities sound so confident and persuasive online, it can be hard to know who to trust. The bottom line is that misinformation spreads much, *much* faster than accurate nutrition advice, so make sure you are relying on professionals who care about your health – not a viral video with millions of views that has popped up on your feed.

UNWANTED SYMPTOMS

For some people, eating more fibre can cause bloating or excess gas, which may lead them to cut back and ultimately minimize their fibre intake. As we know, this is not great news for our overall long-term health. If this is you, then check out page 125 for advice on how to introduce more fibre-rich foods back into your diet while avoiding pesky gas and bloat.

But is it all bad news?

Outside of government guidelines there have been a few initiatives aimed at increasing fibre intake among the public, especially in the UK. As we learn more about just how important fibre is for our health, initiatives such as Action On Fibre have been established to help boost the population's fibre intake. Action On Fibre is an industry-led initiative set up by the Food and Drink Federation and it delivered 118 million additional servings of fibre in 2024 alone – equivalent to 88 million bowls of bran flakes – through collaboration with brands and supermarkets across the country. This has led to reformulations of existing products to boost their fibre content, as well as the introduction of new fibre-rich products to the market.

Similar industry-led movements have emerged in the US, where the first 'Food and Fiber Summit' was held in Washington, D.C., Professionals came together to address the fibre intake gap in the country and discuss solutions. Strategies were proposed to improve public messaging about fibre, educate people on how to read food labels, increase their fibre intake, and correct misperceptions around fibre[148].

Although fibre intake in most countries has not increased in recent years, its popularity is slowly starting to grow. New social media trends like 'fibremaxxing', where people consciously make an effort to maximize the fibre content of their meals, along with fibre becoming more 'trendy', are helping. The rise in research studies on gut health and diet quality is also increasing awareness of fibre's importance, encouraging food manufacturers to create more fibre-rich products to meet increased consumer demand. With more of us talking about fibre, there is hope that our intake in the next few years will start to rise.

As we move into Part 2, you are going to see exactly what foods to eat more of to harness the power of fibre and transform your health. We will also cover easy ways to increase your fibre intake correctly (many people unknowingly get this wrong), and show how small shifts to your plate can make hitting your fibre goals easier than ever before.

Now that you have discovered all the exciting ways that fibre can support your health, you might be wondering, 'Well, how do I start? What do I eat first? How much should I aim for in each meal?' In this part of the book, I will reveal my six steps to help you hit your 30g goal easily each day, as well as the best high-fibre foods to stock up on. I will help you to establish long-term habits to become fibre-focused. Boosting your fibre intake doesn't need to feel like you are going on another diet – how many times have we all tried those with very little success? Think of it as your usual meals and foods you enjoy, with just some gradual tweaks and improvements over time to help you feel and look better!

PART 2

HOW TO MAKE FIBRE YOUR SUPERPOWER

Six Steps to 30g

Although fibre recommendations can vary slightly depending on where you live in the world, my go-to advice for healthy adults is 30g per day. You might already get close to this number, which is fantastic, so take on board all of the principles in this part of the book and try to see if you can boost your intake slightly more to feel even better!

The fibre recommendation in the UK used to be 24g per day[149], but in 2015 this was updated thanks to research showing that this just wasn't enough for optimal wellbeing and disease prevention. Despite this change, there has sadly been very little real increase in the average intake per day (go back to page 59 for a take-down of the reasons why).

Before we hop on the '30g fibre' train, we need to check how much fibre you are currently eating on average (if you suspect you are part of the 90% of us not hitting the recommendations). We touched on some physical signs that you might not be getting enough fibre in Chapter 2, but if you really want to cash in on all the benefits, it is time to do a little number crunching and calculate how much you are getting each day.

Step 1: What to Know Before You Start

How to track your fibre intake

There are a few ways you can track your fibre intake, but I will start with the easiest first. For most people who do not have access to state-of-the-art nutrition databases and technology that nutritionists or dietitians have, food tracking apps can be handy. These apps, such as MyFitnessPal or Nutracheck, can be easy to use on your phone and can tell you your fibre intake after you log each food you eat. The only downside is that some of the data that is found in these apps is user-generated, so it may be slightly inaccurate. To avoid logging incorrect data and getting an inaccurate picture of your fibre intake, choose foods with the green checkmark beside them. These have been verified and are more accurate, but I always recommend double-checking these entries against packaging labels just to be sure. You can also find free fibre calculators online, but again, double-checking against labels is recommended.

If you are a little more old-school and like to write things down, keep a food diary of everything you have eaten that day, with all the exact measurements. Using food labels, you can then add up the fibre content you have eaten that day. However, make sure that you are calculating your fibre intake correctly! Some labels will show the amount of fibre per 100g – not per serving. So, if you're eating 50g or 200g of that food, make sure to adjust the numbers to reflect how much you're actually eating. To get a more representative insight into how much fibre you eat on average, it can be good to track and measure your fibre intake over a week or more. But be warned: most people who do this exercise are pretty shocked at how little they are consuming! By tracking your meals over a few days, you will also start to discover the fibre quantities in your familiar everyday foods, too, which is extremely helpful for sustaining fibre-focused habits long term without having to measure things all the time.

Note: Tracking your food and fibre intake may not be right for everyone. If you have a history of disordered eating, or tracking feels overwhelming, skip this step and just focus on the benefits and physical changes you feel after increasing your intake gradually over a few weeks.

Ensure you are well hydrated

One of the biggest mistakes people make when increasing their fibre intake is that they do not realize the importance of increasing the amount of fluids they drink simultaneously. It is *vital* that as you increase the amount of fibre you consume, you also increase the quantity of water you drink, too. Especially if you drink a lot of coffee, tea or caffeinated drinks, which can be dehydrating, you live in hot weather, or sweat a lot through exercise. Soluble fibre works by drawing water into your intestines, which helps form soft, healthy stools, but if you suddenly increase your fibre intake without staying properly hydrated, it can have the opposite effect, leading to harder stools that are tougher to pass. It's also important to mention alcohol intake. Alcohol is a diuretic, meaning it will increase the amount of fluids lost by your body and cause dehydration. So, if you are drinking regularly and suffer with constipation or gut-health issues, reduce your alcohol intake and/or make sure you are also drinking lots of water at the same time.

HOW MUCH WATER SHOULD WE BE DRINKING EVERY DAY?

Guidelines around how much water we should be drinking each day can be a little confusing. Some recommendations tell us to aim for six to eight glasses of water a day, while others state that around 1.5 litres is enough. However, it has been suggested that for optimal health, and to avoid issues like kidney stones, infections and dehydration, that 2.5 litres of fluid should be consumed if you live in a temperate climate and do mild activity[150]. Fluid intake does not just have to be water – it can include things like teas, juices, milk and sparkling water, too. If you live in a hotter climate, you exercise strenuously and sweat more through this, then you may need to drink slightly more.

Take it slow

Ever heard of the saying 'slow and steady wins the race'? Well, the same principle should be applied to your fibre journey as you look to increase your intake. I often see people realize just how low their fibre intake currently is, then increase their intake far too much in a short space of time – they end up getting bloated and uncomfortable, then think that eating fibre doesn't really work for them. Instead, you just need to go 'low n' slow' – *slowly* increase your fibre intake over time in small amounts. At the start, this might look like adding just a tablespoon or two of beans to your meals for a few days, giving your body time to adjust, and then gradually increasing the amount as you get used to more fibre, for example. Everyone is different, but my general advice is to increase your fibre intake between 1–3g per day until you are eating 30g. If you feel like this is still causing you some issues, go *even* slower and look to boost fibre by 1–2g every two days, for example.

Don't skip meals

When life gets hectic and your schedule is packed, the thought of preparing and sitting down for a meal can seem like the last thing you have time for. But if you are a regular meal-skipper because of lack of time, stress or factors like just not knowing what to eat, then this is your reminder to try your best to carve out time to fuel yourself properly. Not only does skipping meals mean you are more likely to put yourself at risk of vitamin and mineral deficiencies over time, but it also means you are probably going to eat a lot less fibre, too. Meal-skipping can also wreak havoc on blood sugar levels, leaving you feeling tired and sluggish.

But doesn't fasting and intermittent fasting have proven benefits?
The concept of skipping meals or 'fasting' for health reasons has become increasingly popular over recent years. It is true that different types of fasting can provide some benefits to our gut microbiome, improve health outcomes for those suffering with obesity, and offer other benefits like reducing blood pressure in some individuals. However, I often argue that many of these benefits can also come from simply improving the quality of your diet; lowering ultra-processed food intake; reducing excess calories and, of course, boosting fibre intake. If you are struggling with consuming enough fibre each day, then fasting or skipping certain meals may make hitting your recommended intake harder. If you still feel that fasting is right for you, or you practise fasting for cultural or religious reasons, I have outlined a few tips to help you to get enough fibre regardless:

- If your fasting schedule includes skipping one meal, such as breakfast, then it is important to ensure your other meals and snacks during the day are high in fibre. Opting for wholegrains like brown rice, wholegrain bread, and adding nuts, seeds, side salads with high-fibre vegetables, snacking on fruits like apples and green bananas, as well as leaving skins on plants you are cooking (like potatoes and courgettes) can help to boost your fibre intake for the rest of the day.
- Cooking your own meals at home for the times you are not fasting can help you to control and calculate your fibre intake more accurately. Usually, food from fast-food outlets and restaurants can be much lower in fibre due to processing and cooking, so home-cooked food can be a better option during these times.
- During your eating window, make plants the star of your plate – think big salads, portions of wholegrains, extra servings of veggies – and always start your meals by filling up on plant-based foods first.
- Add tablespoons of almond flour, spoonfuls of nut butters or ground flaxseeds to servings of yoghurts, porridge and cereals, or even add them to mixtures if you are baking. These are high in fibre and can make a big difference.
- If you struggle to get enough fibre into your diet around the times you are fasting, a supplement may be helpful. For more advice on fibre supplements, see page 199.

WHAT DOES 30G FIBRE *ACTUALLY* LOOK LIKE?

If you like practical examples when it comes to learning, I have outlined what a 30g of fibre day might look like below. There are also more in-depth example meal plans in Part 3 of this book, which include delicious and easy recipes you can enjoy.

Breakfast
2 thick slices of wholemeal toast (6.6g fibre) with 1 large sliced banana (2g fibre) and 1 tbsp peanut butter (1g fibre)

Lunch
Quinoa salad with salmon and avocado: 185g mixed quinoa (5g fibre), ½ avocado (4.6g fibre), 30g spinach leaves (0.36g fibre) and a salmon fillet

Snack
1 x 15g packet of salted popcorn (1g fibre)

Dinner
Large jacket potato (4.7g fibre) with cheese and 200g baked beans (8g fibre) and a side salad of tomatoes and cucumber (0.5g fibre)

TOTAL FIBRE: 33.7G

Step 2: Re-shape Your Plate to Boost Fibre

Reaching your fibre goals doesn't have to be complicated – just making a few tweaks in terms of how your plate looks can make a huge difference. On a typical plate, protein will often take centre stage, with fibre-rich foods like vegetables and pulses often relegated to the side as an afterthought. Much of this is down to trends in high-protein or high-fat diets like keto, leading to less room for other nutrient- and fibre-dense foods like wholegrains and vegetables. Placing these foods back into the spotlight and making them the focus of our dishes again can not only help you extend your lifespan, but as we know it can also help you lose weight, help slow down ageing, and reduce your risk for many life-threatening diseases. The great news is that you can put these foods back in the spotlight while *simultaneously* doing things like hitting your protein goals for the day, even if you have higher requirements (if you are an athlete, for example, or are recovering from an injury).

To get your golden 30g of fibre each day, the changes to your plate do not need to be *too* drastic. I just want you to shift things around slightly. If the vegetables and/or wholegrains you consume usually take up a measly corner of your plate, or are served separately as a side dish, try to change these proportions. I want you to aim to bulk up the plants and wholegrains on your plate, enough so that around three-quarters of your plate is filled with different varieties of them (try not to just stick to one). Three-quarters of your plate filled with plants doesn't need to mean a boring lettuce salad taking up most of the space – when I refer to plants, this includes beans like black beans, wholegrains such as quinoa, fruit and veg such as kiwis and peas, pulses like lentils, and nuts and seeds such as chia seeds or almonds. It could be a big dollop of hummus (made from chickpeas), roasted and spiced mixed vegetables, a serving of sweet potato and some spicy edamame beans. Or, it could mean most of your plate is filled with a combination of pan-fried broccoli, wholegrain rice and honey-glazed carrots, for example. Get creative and choose and cook plants and wholegrains with heaps of flavour and you will be much more likely to eat and enjoy them.

Do potatoes and wholewheat pasta count towards this?
Potatoes can be included in the 'three-quarters of your plate filled with plants' goal, even if they are technically a starchy carbohydrate and do not count towards one of your 5 a day. Just aim to stick to a portion of up to around 250g (cooked) and then have the remainder consisting of various other types of plant foods. The same applies to wholewheat pasta – just ensure that it is not taking up most of your plate (up to 200g portion) and try to add more plant varieties, such as extra broccoli and aubergine mixed in, which can bulk up your meal.

DO ALL CARBS COUNT?

White bread, white pasta and white rice do not count as wholegrains, so if you are enjoying them, bulk up the rest of the meal with vegetables or other plants that are fibre-rich or, alternatively, swap them for wholegrain alternatives (but still ensure you also have a portion of various other plants on your plate too).

Of course, like anything, there will be times where you don't get these proportions right. As long as you are making the best of an effort you can most of the time try to fill your plate with as many plants as you can, this will make all the difference to your fibre intake.

Can I still hit my protein goals?

One of the biggest misconceptions when it comes to eating a diet filled with more plant foods is that you will miss out on protein. This doesn't have to be the case, even if you are vegetarian or vegan. It is important to fill the rest of your plate with a lean source of protein such as chicken, fish or something like tofu (if you do not consume animal products), but it is important to know that many plant foods, such as beans, also contain protein.

The average person needs to hit at least 0.75g of protein per kg of your body weight per day. So, for example, if you weigh 70kg, work a desk job, and are moderately active and work out a few days a week, a good target for protein intake would be around 53g+ of protein each day. If you are an athlete or are extremely active, then you could increase your intake to around 1.2g protein per kg body weight per day (around 84g of protein). These figures can be achieved while getting your fibre needs at the same time by consuming more of the 'double whammy' foods I have listed out opposite.

'Double whammy' foods (good sources of both protein and fibre)
Although there are many great plant sources of protein, such as the ones listed in the table opposite, it is important to note that many (but not all) plant foods are considered 'incomplete' protein sources. This means they do not contain all nine of the essential amino acids (the building blocks of protein) individually. If you consume animal products you will already be getting these complete proteins in your diet, but if you are vegan or do not consume animal foods, it is a good idea to eat a wide combination of plant foods to ensure you are getting all essential amino acids across different sources.

Additionally, incorporate some of these plant-based foods into your meals, which are among some of the few complete protein sources:

- Quinoa
- Hemp
- Chia seeds
- Edamame beans
- Amaranth

What to eat to meet both your protein and fibre goals

Food	Protein content per 100g	Fibre content per 100g
Edamame beans (cooked)	11.9g	5.2g
Lentils, green (boiled)	8.8g	7.9g
Chickpeas (boiled)	7.6g	7.9g
Tempeh	18g	5.7g
Almonds	21g	10.9g
Chia seeds	17g	34g
Cannellini beans (cooked)	7.4g	6.7g
Black beans (cooked)	6.9g	8.7g
Kidney beans (cooked)	7.8g	6.8g
Quorn or mycoprotein	11g	6g

Breakfast	3-egg omelette with peppers, mushrooms and 1 slice of toasted wholemeal bread with ½ avocado **(27g protein, 9.6g fibre)**
Lunch	Chicken buddha bowl with wholegrain rice, chicken breast, edamame beans, hummus and hoisin mushrooms 1 apple **(56.5g protein, 10.2g fibre)**
Dinner	Beef mince bolognese with kidney beans and wholewheat spaghetti 2 squares of 75% dark chocolate **(46.5g protein, 13.5g fibre)**

Total protein: 130g
(over double of what an average person needs daily!)
Total fibre: 33.3g

The additional benefits of reshaping your plate to boost the fibre content of your meals is that you are more likely to hit your 5 a day because your intake of plant foods will soar. You will also support digestive health by providing more food for your gut bacteria, as we have discussed in Chapter 3. And, lastly, it can make weight management even easier, as many plant foods can be far less calorie-dense than other foods, like those high in fat.

What if I'm on a weight-loss journey?

Losing weight or sticking to a calorie deficit doesn't mean your fibre intake needs to take a hit. In fact, as I mentioned in Part 1, eating more fibre can make weight loss *easier*.

High-volume, low-calorie meals

Load your plate up with heaps of plant foods like spinach leaves, cauliflower, kale, green peas, asparagus and broccoli that are lower in calories but also contain a good amount of fibre. Starchy carbohydrates like bread, potatoes and pasta tend to be higher in calories, so slightly reducing the amount of these you eat each day and replacing them with more vegetables and plant foods can help. Check out a few examples in the diagram below.

How to reduce calories while boosting fibre

Plate of wholewheat pasta with prawns, creamy sauce and a side salad
(8.5g fibre, 528 calories)

→ Reduced pasta portion and more veggies in a garlic dressing
(10g fibre, 467 calories)

200g brown rice
(3g fibre, 264 calories)

→ Half brown rice and half cauliflower rice
(3.5g fibre, 162 calories)

20g mixed nuts
(1.4g fibre, 132 calories)

→ 20g popcorn
(2g fibre, 97 calories)

Steak, butter sauce and a side of sweet potato
(8g fibre, 770 calories)

→ Steak, butter sauce and a side of minty green peas, artichoke and green beans
(9.4g fibre, 690 calories)

Nuts and seeds
When it comes to foods like nuts and seeds, remember that although they are some of the best sources of fibre, they are also very calorie dense. You may want to reduce your intake of these and enjoy them in moderation. Instead of reaching for them throughout the day to snack on, you could try roasting pulses like lentils or chickpeas (see my recipe for Crispy Paprika Chickpeas on page 170) or making popcorn, all of which are high in fibre but less calorie dense. Or enjoy fresh or dried fruit instead.

Be wise with drink choices
When you are in a calorie deficit, it is important not to use up too many of your calories for the day on sugary drinks like energy drinks, specialty coffees or sweetened juices. For example, an iced coffee with whipped cream and added sugar syrup can add an extra 250 calories to your day, meaning that to stay within your deficit your other meals may end up being smaller. On top of that, these drinks can also fill you up, making it harder to eat enough fibre-dense foods throughout the day.

Supplements
Although it is important to try to get all the fibre you need each day from foods first, if you do really struggle with hitting your fibre goals for the day when looking to lose weight, a supplement like inulin or psyllium husk may be helpful. You can add these to water, foods and sauces, or find them in capsules. Part 3 has a more in-depth explanation of the most popular fibre supplements (see page 199). Before taking any new supplements, consult with your doctor, especially if you have a digestive disorder.

Step 3: Get Your Fibre Fix – What to Eat

After doing your calculations in Step 1 (page 74), you might have realized that your current fibre intake is not where it should be. Don't worry, you are not alone. As we know, over 90% of people in countries including the UK and USA are not getting enough fibre in their diets, with only one in three people in the UK even being aware how much they need to be getting in every day[151]. In this section, I will give you a run-down of all the best sources of fibre to start adding to your diet, to make hitting your 30g daily goal feel as easy as pie.

Fibremaxxing

Filling the fibre gap doesn't need to mean eating high-bran cereal every morning or chomping on cardboard-like foods that make you feel miserable. There are much more *exciting* and delicious ways that you can hit your goals, without missing out on your favourite foods. As a nutritionist, I really like to encourage people to improve their diet by focusing on little additions and similar swaps, rather than completely overhauling their diet so it is unrecognisable from before. This makes things more sustainable in the long-term, too. The following tips, swaps and food indexes will give you everything you need to start fibremaxxing in a sustainable way.

DON'T DITCH THE SKIN

Most of us peel fruit or vegetables simply out of habit, but did you know that this peel holds valuable fibre and nutrients that support your health? Peeling a large apple, for example, can reduce its fibre content by up to 1.5g, while removing the skin from a medium potato can reduce its fibre content by half. Peeling fruit and veg can make a big difference to your fibre intake; just think of all the fibre you have missed out on over the years by peeling baking potatoes, sweet potatoes, apples, cucumbers, carrots and even fruits like kiwis – yes, kiwis! One peeled kiwi contains around 2g fibre, but eating a kiwi with the skin still on can boost the fibre content up to 3.5g. I know you might think eating the furry outside coating of a kiwi in order to get your fibre content higher seems a little ludicrous, but eating your kiwis whole in order to boost fibre intake seems to be becoming a popular trend right now, especially as it also lowers food waste! This tip also applies to nuts. Have you ever noticed the brown coating or papery 'skin' around some nuts like Brazil nuts or hazelnuts? This is another great source of fibre and antioxidants[152] not to be missed out on. Try to buy packets of nuts that still have some of this outside brown coating on them (the skin, not the shell!) to boost your fibre intake and add more health-boosting compounds to your diet.

Make some swaps when you shop

Kicking off your fibre-fix journey does not have to mean a total shopping trolley makeover – just little swaps to your regular staple buys can make such a difference.

Instead of:	Switch to:
White bread (1g fibre per slice)	Wholemeal/wholegrain bread (2–3g fibre per slice)*
Cooked white basmati rice (0.6g fibre per 100g)	Cooked wild rice (2.5g fibre per 100g)
Crisps (0.8g fibre per 25g)	Popcorn (3g fibre per 25g)
Milk chocolate (0.4g fibre per 20g)	75% dark chocolate (2.2g fibre per 20g)
White pasta (3g fibre per 150g cooked pasta)	Brown pasta (6.3g fibre per 150g cooked pasta)
Cream crackers (0.7g fibre in a 24g serving)	Rye crackers (3.2g fibre per 24g serving)
White tortilla wraps (1.5g fibre per wrap)	Wholemeal tortilla wraps (3g fibre per wrap)
Juice from concentrate (less than 0.2g per 150ml glass)	Whole fruit options (such as a whole apple, which can contain up to 3g fibre)

* fibre content of foods may vary based on source and processing

Isn't it amazing to see how small swaps like these can boost your fibre intake so much? Especially when it comes to dark chocolate – my personal favourite! Not only do these swaps help us get closer to that 30g daily goal, but many of them contain additional vitamins, minerals and antioxidants that can help to support your health even further. For example, wholegrain bread contains higher amounts of vitamin B6, magnesium, zinc and folic acid because it has not been processed as much, and choosing a dark chocolate compared to milk chocolate can help you get more iron, magnesium and potassium into your diet.

> **WHOLEGRAIN BREAD**
>
> Supermarket wholegrain bread has been demonized a lot recently, due to some of its shelf-prolonging ingredients. However, enjoyed in moderation, they are not harmful to our health and the benefits such as the higher fibre content outweigh the risks. Of course, baking your own wholemeal bread at home instead every day can be better, but realistically most of us do not have the time or resources for this, so picking it up in the supermarket and pairing it with other health-boosting ingredients is absolutely fine.

Fibre claims on food

Food packaging will usually state a product's fibre content, and may highlight a fibre-related claim. In the UK, when a product states it is 'high in fibre', this will mean that it contains 6g of fibre per 100g of the product or 3g fibre per 100 calories. If a product has 3g or more of fibre per 100g it can state 'source of fibre'. For US markets, a product can claim that it is 'high in fibre' if it contains 5g or more of fibre per serving, or contains 20% or more of the daily value of fibre.

For fresh produce in the fruit and veg section that does not usually have a food label, I have added charts on pages 100 and 104, which you can use to help guide you.

Fibremaxx it!

The grids on the following pages show you how to boost the fibre in your diet. They take you through breakfast, lunch, dinner and snack options – you may see favourite recipes you reach for regularly, all given a simple fibremaxx transformation.

Breakfast example:	Fibremaxx example 1	Fibremaxx example 2	Fibremaxx example 3
Porridge	1 tablespoon chia seeds = **+5g fibre** *(chia helps reduce sharp blood sugar spikes and keep energy levels stable throughout the day)*	20g raisins or 15g dried apple pieces = **+1g fibre** *(raisins may contribute to a reduction in LDL cholesterol)*	1 tablespoon psyllium husk = **+5g fibre** *(which can also boost beneficial bacteria in the gut and help with digestion)*
Eggs on toast	200g baked beans = **+8g fibre** *(almost a third of what you need in an entire day!)*	½ avocado = **+4.6g fibre** *(also a source of healthy fats to support brain and hormone health)*	Make your eggs into an omelette with mushrooms and kale = **+1.5g fibre** *(helps provide a good source of vitamin K to help with wound healing)*
Breakfast cereal, such as wheat biscuits or other shredded cereal	60g raspberries = **+ 4g fibre** *(an excellent source of fibre and polyphenols which can help the body protect itself from diseases like cancer)*	20g milled flaxseeds = **+ 4.5g fibre** *(flaxseed is a rich source of vitamin E, antioxidants and niacin)*	1 large banana = **+ 2g fibre** *(bananas contain an array of nutrients like magnesium, potassium and B6 which can help support heart health, mental health and lower blood pressure)*

Lunch example:	Fibremaxx example 1	Fibremaxx example 2	Fibremaxx example 3
Mixed leaf salad with grilled chicken	125g quinoa = + **4.25g fibre** *(quinoa is also a complete source of protein and can help support muscle synthesis and recovery)*	125g spelt = + **5.75g fibre** *(wholegrains consumption, including spelt, is associated with a reduced risk of heart disease)*	½ avocado = **+4.6g fibre** *(15% of your fibre goal for the day!)*
Vegetable soup and a bread roll	80g lentils to the soup = **+6g fibre** *(regular lentil consumption may be linked to improved inflammation responses)*	side salad of grilled artichokes, tomatoes, red onion and spinach = **+3.5g fibre** *(due to their high fibre and antioxidant content, artichokes can support gut health and boost levels of good gut bacteria)*	blend in or add 50g of butter beans to your soup = **+3g fibre** *(butter beans can help with blood sugar regulation due to their low glycaemic index)*
Salmon buddha bowl	portion of Crispy Paprika Chickpeas (see page 170) = **+4.5g fibre** *(may help with weight management and insulin regulation)*	80g sweetcorn = **+2g fibre** *(as well as being high in fibre, sweetcorn is a great source of folate which can be helpful during pregnancy)*	½ portion Roasted Red Pepper and Chilli Hummus (see page 177) = + **2.5g fibre** *(hummus is a great source of fibre to help support digestion and feed your gut bacteria)*

Dinner example:	Fibremaxx example 1	Fibremaxx example 2	Fibremaxx example 3
Shredded beef and veggie stir-fry	sprinkle in a handful of peanuts = **+1.3g fibre** (studies have shown an association between peanut consumption and a reduced risk of cardiovascular disease)	swap rice noodles for 60g buckwheat noodles = **+3g fibre** (buckwheat is a rich source of rutin, which may help prevent the formation blood clots)	switch shredded beef to 75g firm tofu = **+ 1.5g fibre** (tofu is rich in calcium, which supports bone health)
Sushi or a tuna rice bowl	1 tablespoon sesame seeds = **+ almost 1g extra fibre** (sesame seeds are rich in phytochemicals, some of which may possess anti-tumour properties)	swap white rice for brown rice = **+1.2g fibre** (brown rice has been shown in some studies to reduce inflammatory biomarkers and reduce your risk of developing type 2 diabetes)	80g spicy edamame beans = **+4.5g fibre** (regular edamame consumption may help improve symptoms of the menopause)
Chicken pie	80g sweetcorn in the pie filling = **+2g fibre** (sweetcorn contains compounds that may support eye health)	80g buttered peas = **+4g fibre** (alongside fibre, peas are also a great source of protein)	180g side of sweet potato = **+6g fibre** (sweet potato is a great source of carotenoids, which have anti-inflammatory and antioxidant properties)

Snacking example:	Fibremaxx example 1	Fibremaxx example 2	Fibremaxx example 3
Popcorn	20g dark chocolate chunks = **+ 2g fibre** *(dark chocolate consumption may improve blood vessel function and mood, as well as diversity of the gut microbiome)*	portion of Crispy Paprika Chickpeas = **+ 4.5g fibre** *(paprika has been shown in studies to help with managing inflammation in the body)*	15g pecans and 15g dried apple chunks = **2.4g fibre** *(pectin fibre, found in apples, has been shown to help improve gut barrier function)*
Yoghurt pot	1 sliced kiwi = **+2g fibre** *(kiwi consumption may help to improve sleep quality)*	1 tablespoon chia seeds = **+5g fibre** *(chia seeds have been shown to be cardio-protective and help with aiding digestion)*	1 sliced banana = **+2g fibre** *(bananas may help prevent constipation and soften stools)*
Carrot or cucumber sticks	portion of Roasted Red Pepper and Chilli Hummus (see page 177) = **+ 4.7g fibre**	35g black olive tapenade = **+2g fibre** *(olives are a great source of vitamin E and fibre, as well as healthy fats for the brain)*	35g artichoke antipasti = **+ almost 2g fibre** *(artichoke consumption may help with reducing blood pressure)*

The Roasted Mixed Seed Jar

One of my favourite hacks for increasing how much fibre I eat is adding a tablespoon of seeds from my roasted mixed seed jar to most of my meals. A sprinkle of them over a salad, soup, roasted vegetables or a smoothie can add extra flavour while contributing to your fibre intake for the day. I keep these mixed seeds on my counter in a glass jar, so I don't forget to add a tablespoon to my meals. If you add a spoonful to one meal a day over the course of a week, it can lead to an almost 9g increase in fibre. Roasting them is optional – you can just make the mix and use it as is – whatever you prefer. You can also add things like garlic powder and sea salt to the mixture before lightly roasting, or for a sweeter mix, some ground cinnamon.

Fibre per 1 tbsp serving: 1.2g

Ingredients

70g sesame seeds
50g sunflower seeds
75g pumpkin seeds
20g poppy seeds
30g golden linseeds

Method

1. Preheat the oven to 180°C (160°C fan/350°F) and line a baking sheet with baking parchment.
2. Mix all the seeds together in a bowl then spread them out on the lined sheet.
3. Roast in the oven for 10 minutes, then stir and place back into the oven for another 10 minutes until golden, watching carefully that they do not burn.
4. Remove from the oven and allow to cool, then store in an airtight jar for up to a month.

Snack ideas

When embarking on a higher-fibre regime, you might notice that you feel fuller after meals and naturally snack less. But on those days when you need an extra energy boost, there are lots of high-fibre snack options to choose from! In Part 3 we will cover these in more depth, but for now you can check out some of my favourites below. Aiming for snacks to consist of 2–5g fibre can be helpful, but what does that look like?

1 large banana and a tablespoon of peanut butter = 3.5 grams of fibre

½ an avocado on a rice cake = 5 grams of fibre

1 serving of popcorn (20g) = 2 grams of fibre

1 serving of dried mango (40g) = 3 grams of fibre

1 serving of Garlic and Chilli Kale Crisps (see page 168) = 3 grams of fibre

1 serving of 70% dark chocolate (30g) = 3 grams of fibre

Fruit to help you hit your fibre goals

Eating more fruit is one of the easiest ways to consume more fibre, especially since it tastes great! The only downside is that fruit can be a little more expensive to buy fresh, so, as we have discussed earlier, opting for frozen or dried fruit can be a good alternative to keep costs down (see more advice on page 62). In the west, we tend to stick to the same fruits on repeat, such as apples, bananas and oranges, and it can all get a bit tedious after a while, which can impact how much of it we eat. Switch up the fruits you snack on, add to breakfast dishes or pop into smoothies, to make eating healthily a lot more exciting, and you will also get additional fibre and diversity that can help support your gut. Switch out the apples you always put in your weekly shopping trolley for kiwis, or pick a fruit you haven't had recently, maybe papaya or grapefruit, and your gut will thank you.

Opting for fruits like grapes and watermelon that have their seeds still intact can also be a great way to boost your fibre content, as well as keeping all the white pulpy/stringy stuff on bananas and citrus fruits when you eat them – it is bursting with fibre. If you enjoy fruit juices, opt for freshly squeezed options that still have the bits – such as orange juice – instead of smooth alternatives that have the fibre-rich pulp removed. Ideally, eating the whole fruit instead of their juice alternatives is better: for example, 1 large whole apple contains around 2.5g of fibre, while a glass of apple juice may contain only around 0.5g.

When it comes to health benefits, fruit and the fibre it contains has an impressive track record. A series of meta-analyses and systematic reviews reported that increased fruit intake was linked with a 40% reduction in risk of developing Crohn's disease[153,154,155]. Increasing fruit intake has also been linked with reduced risk of being overweight or obese[156,157,158], a reduced risk of death from cardiovascular diseases[159], and a reduced risk of some cancers such as gastric cancer[160]. Another review of several studies found that increased fruit fibre intake was also associated with a reduced risk of developing diverticular disease by 38%[161].

FRUITY FIBRE-ENHANCED FOODS

Many different fruit fibres are utilized to boost the fibre content in food processing. For example, dates and their seeds are used in some breads to boost their fibre while also improving texture and firmness. Unripe banana flour can also be added to foods like cookies, pastas, breads and cakes to boost fibre and texture, too.

Fruit Fibre Index

Here is a grid of the most popular fruits and their fibre content.

Fruit	Fibre content per 100g
Figs (dried)	10g
Dates	8g
Prunes	7.9g
Dried apples	7.6g
Raspberries	6.5g
Dried cranberries	5g
Blackberries	5.3g
Pomegranate	4g
Dried mango	4.5g
Raisins	4.5g
Apples	2g
Oranges	2g
Kiwi	2.7g
Pear	2.6g
Blueberries	2.4g
Papaya	1.8g
Bananas	1.7g
Red grapes	1.3g
Green grapes	1.2g
Pineapple	1.2g
Grapefruit	0.9g
Watermelon	0.5g

In one randomized control trial on subjects with IBS and constipation, subjects who consumed 90g dried figs every day for four months saw significant improvements to their IBS symptoms[162].

In one small intervention study, it was shown that subjects who ate 50g of dates a day for three weeks saw significant improvements in bowel movement and frequency compared to control. These results indicated that regular date consumption may reduce colon cancer risk[163].

Two daily servings of prunes can improve stool frequency and consistency in those suffering with constipation[164,165].

Human intervention studies indicate that consumption of apples is associated with better weight management[166], while it has also been seen that pectin fibre found in apples can help with reducing bad cholesterol[167].

Two portions of kiwi daily can relieve chronic constipation[168,169] and improve bowel function[170] due to its high fibre content.

Power up on veg

In one study that analyzed 30 years' worth of nutrition data from over 100,000 men and women, it was found that eating two servings of fruits and three servings of vegetables in a day could add an additional eight months to our life expectancy[171], with certain vegetables like spinach, kale, broccoli and Brussels sprouts providing the most health benefits[172]. We also know that increasing our intake can reduce our risk of stroke, some cancers, type 2 diabetes and obesity.

Although vegetables may not be on the top of everyone's list of favourite foods, learning different ways to cook them to spruce them up and make them more palatable can help, while also boosting your fibre intake: think honey-roasted carrots, miso-glazed aubergine, or roasted squash topped with goat's cheese. You can also sneak vegetables into almost every dish without knowing they are even there. In Part 3, I have added extra vegetable portions into recipes for dishes including pasta sauces (page 161 for 11-

---

When leaving the skin on fruit and vegetables, wash them thoroughly before consuming. This can not only lower your exposure to bacteria and other pathogens that can cause illness, but it can reduce your exposure to pesticides which can be harmful to your gut. Often, water is not enough to get rid of pesticides, so I soak fruit and veg in a bicarbonate of soda solution: put about 1½ teaspoons in a big clean sink full of clean water, add your fruit and veg and allow to soak for about 12 minutes, then rinse everything well with clean water and pop back in the fridge or enjoy.

Plant Pasta), hummus (page 177 for Roasted Red Pepper and Chilli Hummus) and even sweet treats (page 188 for Dark Chocolate and Avocado Mousse).

A little like fruit, when it comes to veg many of us tend to be creatures of habit: we buy the same vegetables every week from the supermarket and, because we feel a little uninspired, many of them are left to rot in the fridge and are later thrown away. The ones we do buy and consume tend to be lower in fibre, such as carrots, cucumber and tomatoes. Try to give foods like kale a go (see a delicious recipe for Garlic and Chilli Kale Crisps on page 168, which boasts 3g of fibre per portion), or Crispy Paprika Chickpeas (see page 170) which provide 4.5g of fibre per portion. See Part 3 for more recipe ideas, but for many you can enjoy them raw as a snack (like peppers and carrots), too!

Veg Fibre Index

Here is a grid of the most popular veg and their fibre content.

Vegetable	Fibre content per 100g
Artichoke	5.4g
Green peas	5g
Kale	4.7g
Parsnips (boiled)	4.7g
Brussels sprouts	4.5g
Green beans	4.1g
Sweet potato (with skin)	3g
Carrots	3g
Okra	3.3g
Cauliflower	2g
Spinach (cooked and drained)	2.9g
Broccoli	2.8g
Beetroot	2.8g
White cabbage	2.7g
Red cabbage	2.6g
Aubergine	2.4g
Sweetcorn	2.4g
Rocket	2.3g
Leeks (roasted)	2.2g
Red onion	2.2g
White potato (with skin)	2.1g

Vegetable	Fibre content per 100g
Asparagus	1.9g
White onion	1.9g
Peppers (green, red and yellow)	1.8g
Turnip (boiled)	1.8g
Mushrooms	1.7g
Spinach (raw)	1.6g
Celery	1.5g
Courgette	1.3g
Tomatoes	1.3g
Cucumber	0.7g

Due to their high fibre, antioxidant and other health-boosting compounds, artichokes can offer additional support alongside treatment of dyslipidemia, a condition where people struggle with harmful levels of lipids in their blood.

Some studies show that a high intake of cruciferous vegetables like cauliflower and cabbage is associated with a lower risk of colon and lung cancer.

In one US study done on over 12,000 people, it was seen that those who consumed broccoli 1-2 times a week had a 32-43% lower mortality risk compared to those who never consumed broccoli. Of course, other factors come into play, but the data is still interesting to note[173].

Cabbage, in the form of sauerkraut (a fermented cabbage dish), has been claimed to help reduce some symptoms of IBS, as well as helping to improve bowel function.

Wholegrains

Wholegrains are defined as any grain that contains the bran, germ and endosperm. The 'bran' is what gives many wholegrain products such as brown rice, wholewheat pasta, rye bread and quinoa their brown colour, and it is also where you will find most of the fibre content. In more refined grain products like white bread or white rice, the bran and germ are removed and most of the fibre is removed with it.

The structure of unrefined grains

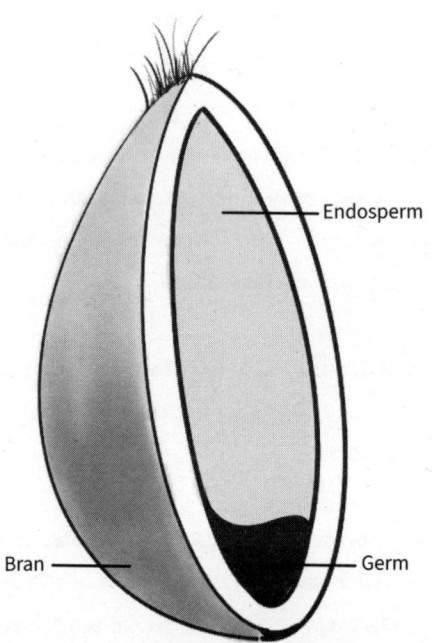

When a grain is refined, the bran and germ is removed, leaving just the endosperm centre.

Switching to more wholegrain sources of food when it comes to preparing meals can make hitting your 30g of fibre a day a *lot* easier. For example, switching white pasta to wholewheat pasta can add 3g of fibre to your plate, and other additions such as quinoa or buckwheat can boost your fibre intake significantly. A higher intake of wholegrains has been shown to be helpful for lowering blood pressure[174], is associated with reducing death rate due to cardiovascular diseases[175] and reducing risk of cancers like colorectal cancer [176].

As we will discuss in Step 6, if you get a little bloated when you eat more wholegrains, you can make changes to how you cook and prepare them to help make digesting them a little easier for your system from the start.

FIBRE SOURCES

At the time of writing, UK adults get just under 40% of their fibre intake from cereals and cereal products, 30% of their fibre from vegetable sources, and 8% from fruit[177]. Cereal products also include wholegrains like rice, bread and pasta. Is this reflective of your own diet? If so, what could you try increasing to make hitting more fibre easier for you?

Wholegrain Fibre Index

Wholegrain	Fibre content per 100g
Oats	10.4g
Wholemeal bread	7g
Rye bread	5.8g
Barley (boiled)	4.9g
Spelt (boiled)	4.6g
Wholewheat pasta (boiled)	4.2g
Quinoa (boiled)	3.4g
Buckwheat (boiled)	2.7g
White bread	2.6g
White pasta (boiled)	2.5g
Wild rice (boiled)	2.5g
Amaranth (boiled)	2g
Brown rice (boiled)	1.5g

A meta-analysis of 28 RCTS showed that 3g or more of beta-glucan fibre found in oats has been shown to reduce bad cholesterol in the body[178] as well as heart disease risk. Beta-glucan fibre in oats may also help reduce blood sugar spikes[179] and keep energy levels more stable.

Studies have shown that when it comes to weight loss, wholegrain rye outperforms both whole and refined wheat food sources, due to its ability to boost satiety and reduce hunger cues.

One randomized control trial done on overweight and obese participants showed that consuming 50g of quinoa a day for 12 weeks reduced serum triglycerides. Elevated triglycerides are linked to an increased risk of developing heart disease.

Increasing your intake of buckwheat may lower cardiovascular disease risk markers such as total cholesterol levels, partly due to its soluble fibre content[180].

Wild rice, due to its high fibre content, can help support the gut microbiome, reduce blood sugar and support digestion. In one animal study, mice who were fed a diet including wild rice for 11 weeks saw a significant boost in levels of beneficial gut bacteria and saw a decrease in the ratio of Firmicutes to Bacteroidetes (which is linked to improved health outcomes).

Beans and legumes

Not only do beans and legumes contain high amounts of fibre, but they are also a source of protein, contain high levels of antioxidants, which can help reduce cell damage, are a source of iron which helps prevent anaemia, and are a source of zinc, which can help support our skin health. Black-eyed beans, chickpeas and lentils are also rich in folate, a nutrient that some of us are currently falling short on. The National Diet and Nutrition Survey showed that between the years 2019 and 2023, 4% of UK adults aged 19–64 had low red blood cell folate levels, but worryingly, 83% of women of childbearing age (16–49) had red blood cell folate levels below the threshold for *maximum* protection against neural tube defects[181]. This means that most UK women who could become pregnant (a time where folate requirements are higher) have an increased risk of their child being born with a neural tube defect. This is also the reason why many women are advised to take a folate supplement and eat more folate-rich beans and pulses before and during pregnancy.

> **EATING FOR LONGEVITY**
>
> It has been found that populations that eat more beans and legumes tend to live for longer, reduce their risk of death by up to 8% for every extra 20g of legumes they eat daily[182], and reduce their risk of developing heart disease[183], type 2 diabetes[184] and colon cancer[185]. In contrast, countries like the US – where bean and legume consumption continues to decline rapidly – now face some of the highest rates of many non-communicable diseases worldwide[186].

Eating more beans not only adds extra flavour and meaty-ness to your plate, but it can also boost the fibre content considerably. For example, adding an extra serving of 60g of edamame beans to your lunch can mean an extra 3g of fibre to your plate (over 10% of your daily fibre goal). Popping just over a third of a tin of lentils into your salad or curry can add an extra 7g of fibre – nearly a quarter of what you need in an entire day! Or you could experiment by adding beans to your sweet baked goods (yes, really!), which can make a huge difference to their fibre content. Check out page 185 for a delicious recipe of bean-boosted brownies that I love to make. If you want to add more of these fibre-filled beans and pulses into your life, check out the table over the page for the ones highest in our favourite nutrient.

I'm scared to add more beans and pulses to my diet – won't that just make me more gassy?
It is true that if you are not used to certain beans and pulses, or you do not prepare them properly, they can cause a little more gas than other foods. This is down to their higher fibre content – specifically types called oligosaccharides, which are poorly digested by humans and can lead to excess gas. This is usually more prominent in the beginning while you are getting used to eating more beans and pulses that are also higher in fibre and can reduce over time as you and your gut bacteria get more used to them. Check out page 126 for more in-depth tips on how to prepare these foods to reduce unwanted gas and bloating.

Bean and Pulses Fibre Index

Beans and pulses (cooked)	Fibre content per 100g
Pinto beans	9.1g
Black beans	8.7g
Chickpeas	7.9g
Green lentils	7.9g
Kidney beans	6.8g
Cannellini beans	6.7g
Red split lentils	6.3g
Butter beans	6.1g
Mung beans	6.1g
Edamame beans	5.2g
Black-eyed beans	4.4g
Green beans (boiled)	4.1g
Baked beans (haricot beans) in tomato sauce	3.9g

Along with its high fibre content, many pulses, including chickpeas, contain an enzyme called alpha-galactosidase, which can also help to improve digestion while also helping to increase bifidobacteria and lactobacilli levels in the gut. This enzyme may also protect the gut from exposure to some carcinogens[187].

One randomized control trial showed that consuming lentils regularly for 12 weeks led to a reduction in cholesterol levels and helped to support the immune system responses[188]. Lentils as part of a balanced diet may also have anti-microbial properties and help with weight management[189].

Edamame beans and other soy products have been shown to slightly reduce menopausal symptoms, according to a meta analysis done using data from over 19,000 women across the globe[190].

Baked bean consumption was shown to reduce serum cholesterol levels in individuals with high cholesterol in one study. For eight weeks, subjects consumed ½ a cup of baked beans (around 120g) daily, and saw significant reductions in their cholesterol levels compared to a control group[191].

Nuts and seeds

After beans and wholegrains, the richest source of fibre is found in nuts and seeds. These are great little additions to any meal or snack, helping to support digestion, providing a source of unsaturated fats that support hormones, brain health and our heart. The fibre content varies across different nuts and seeds, but some of the richest sources (more detail in the chart below) include chia seeds, flaxseeds, poppy seeds, almonds with the skin, pistachios and hazelnuts. Just one handful (around 25g) of nuts such as almonds or hazelnuts can help you hit nearly 10% of your fibre goal for the entire day.

Although a portion of nuts or seeds does not count towards your five a day, it does count towards your plant points and of course your 30g-of-fibre goal each day. I have shared my Roasted Mixed Seed Jar recipe on page 96, but if you struggle to think of more ways to enjoy them, give these tips a go:

- Blend a mix of nuts and seeds in a food processor or blender until they form a fine powder. Mix the powder into your oats in the morning or add to smoothies or when you bake. This is a great way to up the fibre content, while making your foods richer in nutrients.
- Make your own apple and seed porridge to enjoy for breakfast in the mornings. See page 143 for the recipe.
- When you are baking, get creative and try nut-based flours: one of my favourites is almond flour, which can be used in brownies recipes like the one on page 185.
- Use nuts and seeds to make homemade sweet treats. Simple treats like white chocolate-covered Brazil nuts are a great alternative to packaged snacks which are usually devoid of fibre. My

favourite post-dinner treat is my Almond Butter-stuffed Dark Chocolate Dates, which you can find the recipe for on page 182.

ANTIOXIDANT-RICH SKIN

As we touched on in Step 1, leaving the brown skin layer on your nuts (like hazelnuts, Brazil nuts and almonds) can be a great way to boost their fibre content. But did you know that this outer brown coating is where most of the antioxidant content comes from, too? We lose around 50% or more of the antioxidant quantity when we remove it[192], so buying nuts with this brown skin intact can be an even healthier option. Some nuts also go through a process called blanching, which can lower their fibre and antioxidant content further. Choosing roasted nuts can be a great alternative to avoid losing these health-promoting compounds.

Nuts and Seeds Fibre Index

The best fibre-filled nuts and seeds:

Nut/seed	Fibre content per 100g
Chia seeds	34g
Flaxseeds	26.2g
Poppy seeds	19.5g
Almonds (skin on)	10.9g
Sesame seeds	11.8g
Hazelnuts	9.7g
Peanuts	8.2g
Pecans	8.4g
Brazil nuts	8.5g
Sunflower seeds	8.6g
Pistachios	7.4g
Walnuts	6.4g
Pumpkin seeds	5.1g
Cashew nuts	4.1g
Pine nuts	3.7g

Not only are chia seeds incredibly high in fibre and linked to improved digestion, but their consumption may also boost levels of the good kind of cholesterol in the body[193].

In many studies, flaxseed has been shown to help support digestive health. In one study in particular, 50g of flaxseed consumed daily for one month was significant in helping to reduce chronic constipation and bloating in elderly individuals, while also helping to boost the levels of beneficial gut bacteria like Prevotella melaninogenica and Roseburia hominis[194].

Consuming walnuts regularly may help to boost beneficial gut bacteria such as some of the Bifidobacterium genus. One study also showed the 43g of walnuts consumed daily was enough to increase levels of SCFA-producing bacteria that could help boost levels of butyrate and propionate in the body[195] – SCFAs are associated with helping to reduce inflammation and strengthen the gut barrier.

Pine nuts also contain a health-boosting compound called 'pinolenic acid', which may be effective in reducing inflammation and oxidative stress in the body[196].

Step 4: Perfect Your Plant Points

A few years ago, the results of an exciting study called The American Gut Project were released. Using stool samples from over 10,000 people from around the world, the study found that those who ate 30 or more different types of plants (think fruit, veg, nuts, seeds, etc.) per week had the healthiest and most diverse gut microbiomes compared to those who only consumed around ten. As we learned in Chapter 3, having a wide range of gut bacteria can help to boost our immune system, support digestive health and play a role in reducing the risk of certain diseases. The American Gut Project was one of the most influential studies in recent years, as it led to the development of the 'plant points' system, which emphasizes the importance of consuming a variety of different plant foods.

When I tell people about how they should aim to get thirty different plants into their diet per week, most people are a little overwhelmed and feel like it is a little unrealistic. But, as you will see below, it is not just fruits and vegetables that count; wholegrain bread, coffee or tea, and even things like brown rice and pasta all contribute. So, don't let the number '30' scare you – you are probably closer to it than you think!

How do we count 'plant points'?

Counting the plants you eat can be a fun and exciting way to improve your health. Chances are, you will find it much easier to hit your daily 30g fibre goal if you focus on getting more plant foods into your diet using this system. Before you start, there are a few different rules and guidelines to remember:

1. For every different fruit and veg you eat, you get one plant point.
2. Repeat plants do not count as separate points. For example, if you ate a portion of green beans at lunchtime on Tuesday and again on Friday, this only counts as one plant point. Remember: the system is geared towards diversity, so try to shake up the different foods you eat and try new things.
3. Different colours of foods count as different plant points. If you eat a green apple and a red apple in one week, you get two different plant points.
4. Don't go against the grain. Every wholegrain food you eat also counts towards one of the 30 different plant points you need each week. This includes foods like brown rice, quinoa, rye, wholegrain bread, oats and wholewheat pasta.
5. Every different nut and seed you consume in one week counts as one plant point.
6. Don't forget legumes. Many people do not realize that foods like lentils, chickpeas, beans (including baked beans!), butter beans, etc. all count towards one plant point each.
7. Herbs and spices. For each different herb and spice you add into your food, you will get a quarter of a plant point.
8. All servings of plants count towards plant points, regardless of the portion size. However, I recommend eating at least 80g per serving when it comes to different fruits and vegetables, to reap the full benefits and to help boost your fibre intake for that day.
9. Extra-virgin olive oil, coffee and tea each count as a quarter of a plant point.

FROZEN AND TINNED PLANTS

Tinned and frozen plants also count towards a plant point each. Additions like tinned tomatoes to a recipe will give you an extra point, as well as things like frozen mixed vegetables. Unfortunately, fruit and vegetables such as apple juice from concentrate do not count, so aim to stick to whole foods where possible.

Reaching 30 plant points a week (or more!) is an excellent way to expose your gut to a wide variety of different fibres; from cellulose to beta-glucans, to lignin and pectin, helping you gain the benefits that are associated with each. If you feel 30 plants a week seems like too far a stretch from what you currently eat, then aim for 20 and build your way up slowly, trying different foods and recipes to help you.

Top tips to help you boost your plant points

Eat the rainbow
Remember that different colours of fruit and vegetables count towards different points each week. Instead of buying a multipack of six green apples, opt for a mixture of loose green and red apples, or choose a variety of purple and sweet potatoes, for example. Not only does eating a wider range of plant colours help you bump up your plant points, it also means you get in a wider range of different types of health-boosting phytonutrients, like 'anthocyanins', found in purple and red plants, which can slow down cell ageing[197], or carotenoids, which give plants an orange colour and can help tackle free radicals that can cause damage to the body.

Switch up your salad bags
One of the easiest ways to boost your plant varieties is by switching your salad leaves up to a variety pack. Instead of a bag of spinach leaves or lettuce, opt for mixed leaves.

Bulk up your meals with plants
Adding portions of tinned lentils into pasta sauces or curries, popping a spoonful of beans into salads or topping your soups with crunchy nuts and seeds can add extra points to help you hit your weekly goal. One of my favourite examples of this is my hearty Lamb, Lentil and Sweet Potato Shepherd's Pie which you can find on page 162. This can also help to lower the cost of these meals.

Hidden veg sauces
One of my favourite ways to add more plant points as well as fibre into my diet is by blending cooked vegetables into sauces for dishes like pasta (see page 161 for a recipe). Adding some cauliflower, white beans or cooked mushrooms into a blender with your sauce of choice – for example – can also add flavour and extra nutrients to your dish!

Don't underestimate the power of spices
Although they only equate to a quarter of a plant point, adding different combinations of spices to your meals and drinks can all add up and make a difference. Try adding a sprinkle of cumin and turmeric to a soup you are enjoying at lunchtime, some cinnamon to your coffee or porridge bowl, or dust some paprika and chilli powder over your vegetables before you roast them in the oven. It all adds up!

Sweeten foods with fruit
Adding fruit like dates, mangoes or apples to things like smoothies and pancakes can be a great way to sweeten them while boosting plant points and fibre. I also like to suggest little switches such as adding fruit instead of honey to yoghurt bowls; perhaps opting for some chopped kiwi and raspberries instead – helping to take your yoghurt bowl from zero to two plant points, too!

Swap your snack choices
Switching out some of your regular snacks for ones that are more abundant in plants can be a game-changer. If you love to snack on hummus and breadsticks, use carrot or cucumber sticks instead. Or, if you enjoy a chocolate bar in the evenings, switch this to a multiseed and nut bar with chocolate chips in it. Remember, small swaps make all the difference!

Diversify what you eat
If you feel that your fibre intake is low and you struggle to get anywhere close to 30g a day, then start diversifying the foods and meals you eat and trying new foods and ingredients. This is also a helpful way to support your gut microbiome, because consuming a wide range of different fibre from different foods is just as important as the quantity you consume each day. I always recommend that clients try out new cuisines, as usually this opens them up to new foods that can be full of fibre and keep things exciting. Foods like plantain, yams, mung beans, edamame beans and okra are all great examples and are versatile and fibre-rich, too!

During your weekly food shop, challenge yourself to pick up one new ingredient a week from the fruit and vegetables section (or from beans, nuts, seeds or wholegrains!) that you have not tried before or eaten recently, and try out a new recipe with it. This will help to make cooking healthy fibre-filled meals exciting again while also helping you get a wider range of different types of fibre into your diet.

Meal-prepping
Diversifying what we eat can be a little challenging when you are a creature of habit, especially if you are someone who likes to prepare your week of meals in advance. Batch-cooking one meal for the entire week can definitely make life easier, but eating the same thing every day can limit your fibre intake and diversity.

When meal-prepping, try to:

- Batch-cook 1–3 different recipes for the week, filled with at least three different types of plants.
- Try to ensure the batch-cooked dishes you are preparing in advance have at least 10g of fibre in them per portion, such as my Easy Bean and Veg Stew (page 155), or the Mexican-inspired Beef and Black Bean Bowl (page 156).
- Prepare snack-packs you can enjoy alongside these meals. These can be portions of dried fruit, trail mix, mixed nuts or multigrain crackers.

Step 5: Overcoming Fibre Frustrations

You should now feel much more acquainted with fibre: you know what it is and why it's good for you, how much you need to be eating every day, and you should be more clued up on what foods you need to add to your diet to make boosting your intake a lot easier (if you need a recap, go back to Steps 3 and 4). But knowing what to eat is only half the battle – how your body reacts to those changes matters, too. One of the most common objections I hear when I tell people to boost their fibre intake is that fibre makes them bloated, constipated and/or sluggish, so let's cover what to do to avoid these teething issues as you embark on your fibre-filled journey.

WHAT IS BLOATING?

You may have experienced it yourself after a large meal, or perhaps when you have eaten a little too quickly. Your stomach extends and feels a little 'swollen'. A little bit of bloating after a meal is perfectly normal and it is natural for your stomach to expand slightly as the day goes by, but if this bloating is persistent, visible even before you have eaten anything, or is painful, then this is not normal, and I recommend getting checked out by your doctor.

Why do we feel bloated?
Eating more fibre and plant foods – especially if we are not used to them – can lead to a shift in the gut microbiome. With more fuel for our gut bacteria to feed on and ferment, they then get stronger, multiply and more diverse varieties of them populate our gut. This

can often then lead to more gases being produced, which unfortunately can mean more bloating for some people. The good news is that our bacteria adjust over time, and these symptoms usually don't last for too long. Powering through and using the tips in the next section can help reduce discomfort.

How do I avoid symptoms of bloating and constipation when I start eating more fibre?

Slow and steady
As mentioned in Step 1, don't ramp up your fibre intake too quickly. Instead, aim to build it up gradually until you reach the golden 30g-a-day guideline. There is no 'set' pace, but aim to increase your fibre intake by between 1g and 3g per day, or slower if you are finding it harder to adjust. Increasing the amount of fibre you eat slowly is important as it gives your beneficial gut bugs time to adapt, meaning you will be less likely to suffer from bloating and excess gas.

Play around with different foods
Feeling bloated or sluggish after upping your fibre intake might have more to do with *where* your fibre is coming from than how much you're eating. In the early days of adjusting your intake, it can help to ease yourself in by swapping some of the higher-fibre foods like chia seeds, flaxseeds, or certain cruciferous veggies like broccoli, for gentler options like carrots or tomatoes – but you may need to eat more of these (in volume) to make up for the gaps in fibre intake. As your gut adjusts, you can slowly add in more of the higher-fibre options you removed, little by little, testing which foods work for you and which ones do not.

Stay hydrated
Another reason why you might feel a little backed up or bloated after eating more fibre is due to your hydration levels. As I mentioned in Step 1, fibre absorbs water in the intestines, adding bulk to stools and making it easier for food to pass through your digestive system and out the other end. The more fibre you eat, the more water is needed for the digestive process. Being dehydrated can lead to drier, harder stools and constipation. To prevent feeling backed up and bloated, drink water regularly throughout the day to keep things moving along nicely.

Munch your way to better digestion
One of the biggest culprits that causes bloating, indigestion, trapped gas and even constipation – especially when consuming higher-fibre foods – is when they are not chewed well enough. Our busy lifestyles can mean we tend to eat on the go and rush our meals, or we don't pay enough attention to how we eat. Although there is no 'set' number of times you should chew each bite, aim to keep munching away until food becomes a 'paste-like' consistency before swallowing.

Prepare and cook your fibre-rich foods properly
Soaking, rinsing and cooking certain plant foods that are high in fibre can help with digestion, reducing unwanted symptoms. This is especially helpful if you have a sensitive gut, or you are elderly.

- Soak foods like oats, chia seeds, beans, lentils and even some nuts, in water to help to make them easier to digest, especially while your gut adjusts to the increase in fibre consumption. How long you need to soak them will depend on the food.
- Soak dried beans and lentils overnight, or for at least six hours, before cooking. This will help your system digest them more easily.
- During the boiling process of foods like lentils and chickpeas,

remove the foam that forms on the top of the water while cooking, as this has been thought to help reduce gas formed by bacteria during digestion.
- Rinsing foods like dried chickpeas and lentils well under cold running water before soaking or cooking them can help to remove intestine-irritating particles like dirt, while also removing some of the indigestible carbohydrates that can cause gas and bloating. I also recommend rinsing tinned beans and pulses before eating them, while your gut adjusts to them, if they haven't previously been a feature in your diet.
- Cooking beans, lentils and foods like dried peas twice has been a practice long used in countries like Greece, to help with reducing gas and discomfort post-meal. After rinsing, add your beans or pulses to a saucepan and boil for around 10 minutes, then drain away this water, replace it with fresh water and cook again until tender.
- Sprouting pulses can be a great way to still enjoy them, with less gas. You can buy pre-sprouted pulses in most supermarkets or make these yourself at home.
- Some claim that cooking beans and pulses in a pressure cooker helps make them more digestible. If you have a pressure cooker, experiment by using it to cook some of the beans and pulses in the recipes at the back of this book, and see if it makes a difference.

What if I have IBS?

Irritable Bowel Syndrome is a condition that affects the digestive system, usually causing uncomfortable abdominal symptoms such as excess bloating, pain, constipation or diarrhoea. It is known that foods very high in fibre – especially insoluble fibre – may trigger symptoms in many people with IBS, so it is recommended to focus on getting more soluble fibre-rich foods into the diet instead. Foods rich in soluble fibre such as oats, carrots, ripe bananas and apples, can be easier on the digestive system as they absorb water, forming a gel-like substance that makes it a little easier for them to pass through a more sensitive gut.

If you have IBS, not getting enough fibre can worsen your symptoms – but increasing your intake needs to be done slowly and carefully. While it is never a good idea to increase your fibre intake too fast, this is especially important for those who have IBS, as their gut can be a little more sensitive to sudden changes. Elimination diets such as the low-FODMAP diet (see below) may be helpful short-term steps to help you manage symptoms, build up tolerance to different types of fibre, as well as help you identify your triggers, but should be only done under the supervision of a dietitian.

Generally, it is recommended that those with IBS ensure they are well hydrated each day, they do not skip meals, they reduce their caffeine intake, cut down on fatty and fried foods such as fast food and ready meals, and sweet foods like cakes and biscuits, as well as manage stress. Depending on your symptoms, you may be asked to reduce high-fibre foods for a short period of time, or even add in a probiotic supplement, but working closely with a qualified professional will help you to figure out what is right for you.

Could lowering my intake of high-FODMAP foods help me with my symptoms?

Some fibre-rich foods may also contain higher levels of things called 'FODMAPs', which for some people can exacerbate symptoms like bloating and excess gas – especially if you suffer with IBS (Irritable Bowel Syndrome) as mentioned in the section above, or SIBO (Small Intestinal Bacterial Overgrowth). FODMAP stands for 'Fermentable, Oligosaccharides, Disaccharides, Monosaccharides and Polyolys', and these are short-chain carbohydrates found in higher levels in foods like onions, leeks and kidney beans. Consuming a low-FOD-MAP diet can temporarily help to reduce symptoms for those with a more sensitive gut, but this should not be a long-term solution as it can mean lower fibre intake and less plant diversity – bad news for your gut health.

Food	High-FODMAP content	Low-FODMAP alternatives (that mostly contain a good source of fibre)
Fruits	Apples, ripe bananas, goji berries, plums, prunes, figs, apricots, watermelon	Bananas, blueberries, seeded grapes, strawberries, pineapple, oranges, raspberries
Vegetables and pulses	Leeks, onion, garlic, artichokes, green peas, kidney beans, cauliflower, butter beans, chickpeas	Carrots, beansprouts, white potato, green beans, spinach, tomatoes, courgette, aubergine, sweetcorn, broccoli heads, quinoa, oats
Nuts and seeds	Cashews, pistachios	Almonds, chia seeds, sunflower seeds, pumpkin seeds, peanuts, pecans

If you feel like eating many of the high-FODMAP foods from the list above leads to uncomfortable gastrointestinal symptoms for you, doing a short-term low-FODMAP diet (guided by a dietitian) can be a helpful way to remove and then reintroduce these foods back into your diet to help you tolerate them better. You can also switch some of these high-FODMAP foods out with low-FODMAP high-fibre alternatives from the right-hand side of the table.

Important note: If you are suffering with excess consistent bloating, abdominal pain, blood in your stool, constipation, loose stools or any other symptoms, it is important to speak to a medical professional.

Step 6: Stay on Top of Your Fibre Game

As the saying goes, 'habits are only as good as the ones that stick', so in this section we are going to talk all about how you can ensure you stay consistent with your new fibre-focused habits in the *long term*. This will give you the best shot at reducing disease risk, supporting your gut microbiome and reaping all the wonderful benefits that fibre can give us. At the beginning of your new higher-fibre lifestyle, you might benefit from a clear plan telling you *exactly* what meals to eat, so in Part 3 of this book I have outlined a few different meal plan examples and heaps of different fibre-filled recipes for inspiration, to ensure you set off on the right foot. I recommend you follow these meal plans for at least four weeks, because building new habits can take anywhere between 21 and 66 days to form.

Plan ahead and get organized

The concept of planning ahead may seem a little tedious, but as we touched on in Chapter 1, planning and preparing meals in advance is worth the extra effort. When you have an idea of the meals you are going to prepare at home for the week, you have a better chance of being able to figure out your fibre intake and fill in any gaps. Planning meals in advance and staying organized long-term helps you avoid having to eat out or grab food in places like fast-food outlets as often. Most meals found in fast-food establishments are low in fibre and plants, so relying on them for a lot of your meals can make hitting your fibre goals harder. Once you get into the swing of planning meals in advance, it will become second nature to you and this will help build long-term healthy habits.

If you are eating out, try incorporating some of the tips below to help keep your fibre intake on track:

- Try not to fill yourself up too much with pre-meal snacks like white bread, which is lower in fibre, and leave some space for the main event and fibre-rich sides.
- Main meals in restaurants are usually based around meat, so if you choose one of these, add some plant-based sides. A side of Tenderstem broccoli can add an extra 3g of fibre to your main meal, or how about adding on a portion of creamed spinach, which can provide 2–3g of extra fibre?
- If choosing a lower-fibre main meal, you can also bulk up your fibre by choosing a starter such as a vegetable soup or a bean dip, for example, both of which can be a great source of extra fibre.
- Don't forget that many desserts can also be a source of fibre! Apple or berry crumbles or treats like rice pudding can be a delicious and sweet treat that also contain some of our favourite nutrient – but enjoy these in moderation due to their sugar content!
- Lastly, if it feels too challenging to reach your fibre target when you are eating out, don't worry — remember, this is just an aim and if there are some days you fall slightly below target then you can always just get back on track the day after.

Get to know your fibre foods

As they say, education is power. Use this book to build your knowledge on the fibre content of the foods you eat to encourage you to make more long-term fibre-forward swaps. For example, if you know that a side of white rice only provides 0.6g of fibre, but a side of quinoa helps you get an extra 3.4g of fibre, you will be more likely to choose the higher-fibre option because of the health benefits you've learnt in this book. Being educated on the fibre content of your favourite meals and snacks also helps to make hitting your fibre intake a lot more achievable, more sustainable and less overwhelming.

Make it a family affair
Getting other people at home involved with your new higher-fibre regime will make sticking to it long-term a lot easier. Share high-fibre meals, talk about the benefits of fibre and keep yourself accountable with someone else at home to help ensure you stay on the right track. This new higher-fibre lifestyle is not another fad diet, and should be seen as a new way of eating that will positively impact the health of everyone at home, not just you! We know that it is not just adults who have low fibre intake – children often do, too. Only around 4% of children in the UK between the age of 11 and 18 are currently meeting fibre recommendations[198], with over 95% of children in the USA not hitting their fibre recommendations daily[199]. So if you have children, shifting your meals so that they include more fibre will help them, too.

Note: Fibre recommendations for children will be less than those for adults. For recommended intakes, check your specific country's guidelines.

Rearrange your kitchen
One of the ways I have kept on top of my fibre game for so long is because I have made high-fibre foods much more physically accessible and easier to see in my kitchen. This makes me far more likely to cook recipes using them, as well as snack on them. For example, I make sure I always have a fruit bowl filled with higher-fibre fruits (like bananas, apples and kiwis) on my countertop for easy snacking instead of hidden in the back of the fridge. I have rearranged the counter beside my stovetop and keep foods like dried wholegrain

rice, oats, dried lentils and a big jar of mixed seeds there, for easier access, instead of hiding them away in the back of the cupboard. This makes me much more likely to cook with them and enjoy them regularly!

Experiment with a more plant-based diet
In Step 4 (see page 118), I mentioned the concept of trying things like meat-free Mondays and experimenting with more plant-based options. Reducing your meat and animal products intake can significantly boost the amount of fibre you consume as plant foods take their place, helping to support your health and longevity. There are also many meat-replacement products that are a source of fibre, such as tempeh, tofu and quorn. Making it a habit in your household to commit to one completely plant-based day a week (Mondays or not!), adding more plants into your favourite recipes to bulk them up, or switching out some of the snacks you buy (such as beef jerky or string cheese) for things like mixed nuts or crispy seeds can be new habits that make hitting your fibre goals much easier.

Set goals
Set clear and realistic goals to help you stay on track long-term. Start off by aiming for 30g of fibre per day and 30 plants a week – following the recipes and meal plans in Part 3 will make this easier, especially at the start. Once you achieve this consistently, you will find that hitting all other health goals, such as '5 a day' or even reducing your calorie intake will become a lot easier, too. You could even set up a sticker or reward chart in your kitchen with everyone else in your household, with those hitting the most plant points and their fibre goals consistently winning a prize or being able to take a few days off household chores! Get creative and make hitting your goals as fun as possible.

Managing those low-fibre days

There are going to be days where getting enough fibre in your diet may feel a little harder than others – for example, if you are sick, travelling, or life just seems especially hectic that day. Life sometimes gets in the way of our goals, but just get back on track as soon as you can to ensure that you stay as consistent as possible and do not fall off the wagon permanently.

When you are travelling, you can do the below to ensure you are getting enough fibre while supporting your digestion, too:

- If you are flying, it is important to drink enough water (even more than usual), as aeroplanes are very dehydrating. This dehydration can cause excess bloating and digestive issues, especially if you are eating high-fibre foods. Avoid caffeinated drinks and alcohol, which also have dehydrating effects on the body.
- Stay organized and prepare your own meals and snacks for your journey: this will help ensure you are fuelling yourself with adequate nutrition while also meeting your fibre goals. Most airlines allow you to take meals through security (it is just liquids you cannot bring through), so this can help you to avoid the low-fibre snacks and meals available in the airport/bus/train terminals. Most plane meals or snacks are low in fibre, very high in salt, and often consist of ultra-processed ingredients which can make you feel worse. In terms of snacks, foods like dried or fresh fruit, nuts and seeds are all great snack options that are high in fibre and micronutrient -rich.
- If you can't prepare and take your own meals on your journey and have to go for plane or train food, opt for the vegetarian option, if possible. When I fly, I find that the vegetarian options I choose are much more plant-dense, with healthier wholegrains, compared to the other options. This can be super helpful in ensuring you are

getting enough fibre when travelling, to support your digestive system, which may have taken a hit from your journey.

If you are sick, it is important to support your body in your recovery as best you can. This includes getting in enough fibre.

- Enjoy easy-to-digest vegetable soups (which you can blend and add beans and seeds to) as they are easier on your system.
- Pair soups with a wholegrain or seeded loaf, to boost the fibre intake of the meal further.
- Smoothies are another great way to boost your fibre and nutrition intake and are delicious and easy to prepare. Add extra portions of seeds and even higher-fibre veggies like spinach or cooked cauliflower (yes – cauliflower! It adds a creamier texture to smoothies) to them to support digestion – this will also help feed and regenerate some of the beneficial gut bacteria you may have lost while being unwell, and help to bind and remove toxic waste from your system.
- A supplement may also be useful to help boost your intake and get you back on track, but it is important to check with your doctor before using supplements, especially if you have been unwell. For more information on fibre supplements, check out page 199.

If you have had a prolonged period of time where healthy eating has taken a back seat, then your fibre intake has probably suffered, too. If it feels like a while since you last consumed 30g a day, increase your intake gradually. Boosting your fibre intake slowly but surely can help you to avoid any unwanted symptoms (as we talked about in Part 2). If you have just had one day of low fibre, then you do not need to double your fibre intake the next day to make up for it. Just get back on track and commit to staying consistent with healthier eating habits to hit your 30g.

Recap of why fibre matters

As we wrap up this chapter and move into the practical recipes and meal plans, I want to leave you with one final reminder of why maintaining fibre-focused habits for the long-term matters so much – and give your motivation a fresh boost before we head into Part 3.

Remember, fibre is one of the best tools in your health toolbox when it comes to boosting longevity, helping you age more slowly, supporting digestive health and reducing disease risk. A long-term high-fibre diet is associated with:

- Reducing the risk of many kinds of cancer, including colon and breast cancer.
- Lowering cholesterol and supporting heart health. High-fibre diets can also reduce the risk of developing or dying from cardiovascular diseases, which claim millions of lives every year. If you have a family history of CVDs, staying on top of your fibre intake is particularly important.
- Reducing the risk of mental health disorders[200,201,202]. Around half of the world's population will experience at least one mental health disorder by the age of 75[203], so boosting your fibre intake and improving your diet may provide protective benefits or help manage mental health disorders better.
- Supporting brain health. Higher fibre intake may reduce the risk of developing diseases like Alzheimer's, and help improve cognitive function, boosting your focus so you can be more productive at work or sharpening your critical-thinking skills.

Increasing your fibre intake can also positively affect your skin, energy, mood, weight and much, much more. The key is consistency: make your high-fibre regime a life-long habit that you commit to, not just a few weeks' effort!

If you are ready to look your best and feel amazing, then head into Part 3 to start your Fibre Fix journey with all of the delicious recipes, snack ideas and easy-to-follow meal plans!

By now you will have all the knowledge of just how powerful fibre is for your health, where to find it, how much you need and how to increase your intake gradually. Now, it's time for the fun part! In this section, I will show you delicious, practical ways to put everything you have learnt into action – with gut-boosting, high-fibre recipes and snacks you can enjoy, as well as example fibre-focused meal plans you can follow to start you off strong. If you have not read Parts 1 and 2 yet, I urge you to head back and read these sections first before turning the page.

PART 3
RECIPES AND MEAL PLANS

Breakfast

Starting your day off with a balanced, fibre-filled breakfast will help you set the tone for the rest of the day and encourage you to stick to healthier choices. In this section, I have included a mixture of savoury and sweet options, so whatever mood you are in there is something to hit the spot. Remember that skipping breakfast will impact your fibre intake for the day and make it harder for you to hit your daily 'golden 30' – so try to ensure you leave enough time in the mornings or the night before to prepare.

Green Goddess Shakshuka

SERVES 4 • **FIBRE PER SERVING: 7G** • **PLANT POINTS: 9** • **VEGGIE**

drizzle of olive oil

160g trimmed leeks, finely chopped

60g curly kale, finely chopped

½ tsp garlic powder

50g okra, roughly chopped

60g spinach leaves

4 spring onions, chopped

a few coriander stalks, chopped, plus extra leaves to serve

juice of ½ lime

200g passata

40g tomato purée

5g basil leaves, plus extra to serve

130g tinned, drained butter beans

2 tsp harissa paste, plus extra to serve

45ml water

4 eggs

salt and pepper

4 slices of sourdough bread, toasted, to serve

1. Heat the oil in a large saucepan over a medium heat, add the chopped leeks and kale and fry for 1 minute, then add the garlic powder, okra, spinach, spring onions, coriander and lime juice and fry for 2 minutes, then add the passata, tomato purée, basil, drained butter beans, harissa and water to the pan. Stir well to combine.

2. Make 4 wells in the mixture to make space for the eggs. Crack an egg into each well then put the lid on the pan and cook for about 4 minutes until the egg whites are cooked through and the yolks are still runny. Season with a little salt and pepper.

3. Garnish with extra coriander and basil leaves and serve drizzled with harissa paste, accompanying each portion with a slice of warm sourdough toast.

Warming Apple and Cinnamon Oats

SERVES 1 • **FIBRE PER SERVING: 10G** • PLANT POINTS: 4½ • VEGGIE

1 red or green apple

50g rolled oats

1 tsp chia seeds

7g milled flaxseed

½ tsp mixed spice

100ml milk of your choice

100ml water

1 tsp coconut oil

¼ tsp ground cinnamon

runny honey, for drizzling (or agave syrup, if vegan)

1. Cut the apple in half, removing the seeds and the core. Set one half aside, then grate the other (including the skin!) using the coarse side of a box grater.

2. Add the grated apple together with the oats, chia seeds, flaxseed, mixed spice, milk and water to a saucepan and place over a medium-high heat. Stir well and cook for 2–3 minutes until piping hot, then set aside to cool slightly while you make the apple topping.

3. Chop the other half of the apple you set aside earlier into small chunks. Add these apple chunks to a separate non-stick saucepan with the coconut oil and ground cinnamon. Mix well and fry over a medium-high heat for about 2 minutes until softened, then remove from the heat.

4. Serve your porridge in a bowl and top with the cooked apple chunks, then finish with a generous drizzle of honey and enjoy!

5-Minute Smoky Baked Beans on Toast

SERVES 2 • **FIBRE PER SERVING: 10G** • PLANT POINTS: 2 • VEGAN

1 x 400g tin butter beans, drained

200g tinned finely chopped tomatoes (or passata)

1 tbsp tomato purée

1 tsp smoky BBQ seasoning

1 level tsp brown sugar

1 tsp balsamic vinegar

1 large pinch of salt

2 slices of sourdough bread, toasted, to serve

1. Put all the ingredients in a saucepan and place over a medium-high heat. Mix well and cook, stirring regularly, for about 3 minutes.

2. Serve with the toasted sourdough and enjoy.

Banana, Chia and Raspberry Pancakes

SERVES 2 • **FIBRE PER SERVING: 7.1G** • PLANT POINTS: 4 • VEGGIE

40g rolled oats

10g chia seeds

1 large ripe banana, peeled

20g raspberries

1 tbsp honey

30ml plant milk

2 eggs

drizzle of melted coconut oil

To serve

2 tbsp coconut yoghurt

50g raspberries

runny honey, for drizzling

1. Put the oats, chia seeds, peeled banana, raspberries, honey, plant milk and eggs in a blender and blend well until smooth.

2. Place a small non-stick frying pan over a medium heat. Add the coconut oil, then a small spoonful of pancake batter, and fry for 1–2 minutes on each side, flipping when you see the middle of the pancake start to bubble. Remove the cooked pancake, set aside on a plate and continue cooking the rest of the batter.

3. Once all pancakes are cooked, divide them between two plates and top each portion with a tablespoon of coconut yoghurt, 25g raspberries and a drizzle of honey.

Courgette Fritters with Poached Egg and Avocado

SERVES 3 • **FIBRE PER SERVING: 8G** • PLANT POINTS: 5½ • VEGGIE

250g courgettes

1 spring onion, trimmed and very finely chopped

8g dill fronds, finely chopped, plus a little extra to serve

10g mint leaves, finely chopped

1 garlic clove, crushed

juice of ½ lemon

100g Greek feta cheese

7 large eggs

50g plain flour

extra virgin olive oil, for frying and drizzling

1 tbsp distilled malt vinegar

2 avocados, peeled, stoned and sliced

salt and pepper

chilli flakes, to serve

1. Cut the ends off the courgettes then grate them using the larger holes on your grater. Place the grated courgette in a clean muslin cloth, wrap it up and squeeze the cloth tightly to remove as much of the water from the grated courgette as you can. Put the courgette in a large mixing bowl.

2. Add the spring onion, dill and mint to the bowl of courgette along with the crushed garlic, lemon juice and a large pinch of salt. Crumble in the feta, add 1 egg and combine well, then mix in the flour.

3. Heat 4 tablespoons of extra virgin olive oil in a non-stick frying pan over a medium-high heat and while it heats up, boil the kettle.

4. Spoon a heaped tablespoon of the fritter mixture into the pan and flatten each dollop of mixture well. Fry for about 2 minutes on each side, flipping them carefully with a spatula, until golden on each side. Repeat until all the fritter mix is used up, transferring each cooked fritter to a sheet of kitchen paper on a plate to the side to cool slightly and so the excess oil can be absorbed.

5. As the last few fritters cook in the pan, pour the boiling water from the kettle into a separate saucepan and add the vinegar. Carefully break 4 of the eggs into separate ramekins, then carefully and gently tip them one at a time into the boiling water. Bring to a simmer and poach them for a few minutes until they reach your desired 'runniness'. Using a slotted spoon, transfer the first 4 poached eggs to a plate while you cook the remaining 2.

6. Serve 2 fritters with 2 poached eggs on each portion, along with half a sliced avocado. Sprinkle each serving with chilli flakes and more chopped dill, season with salt and pepper and drizzle with a little olive oil.

Main Dishes

The recipes in this section are heavily influenced by Mediterranean flavours and ingredients – particularly those associated with Greek food. Being half Greek, I have always had a passion for the meals from this region – many of them are naturally filled with fibre, flavour and nutrients that help to nourish our bodies. There is a mixture of warming recipes that can be enjoyed on colder days, and lighter ones that curb your appetite when you are looking for something satisfying but not too heavy. Many of these mains can also be enjoyed with the side dishes from pages 173–179.

Creamy Bean and Leek Orzo

SERVES 4 • **FIBRE PER SERVING: 8G** • PLANT POINTS: 8¼ • VEGGIE

generous drizzle of olive oil, plus extra to serve

1 white onion, diced

3 garlic cloves, crushed

1 leek, trimmed and sliced

115g chestnut mushrooms, sliced

35g spinach leaves

800ml vegetable stock (I use 1 vegetable stock cube)

1 x 400g tin butter beans, drained

juice of ½ lemon

small bunch of thyme, leaves removed and chopped, plus extra to serve

250g orzo

2 tbsp jarred capers, drained

80ml single cream (or coconut milk, if vegan)

30g vegetarian hard cheese or Parmesan, grated (optional, omit if vegan)

salt and pepper

1. Heat the olive oil in a large saucepan over a high heat, add the onion, garlic, leek and mushrooms and fry for 2 minutes, stirring regularly, then add the spinach and cook for 1 more minute until the spinach has wilted.

2. Add the vegetable stock, drained butter beans, lemon juice, thyme, orzo and capers to the pan, bring to the boil, season with salt and pepper, then reduce the heat and simmer for 10–12 minutes, until the orzo is cooked, stirring regularly.

3. Turn off the heat, add the cream and Parmesan (if using) and stir to combine.

4. Serve in bowls with extra thyme, a drizzle of olive oil, more Parmesan and plenty of cracked black pepper.

Cod with Tomato and Caper Lentils

SERVES 4 • **FIBRE PER SERVING: 12G** • PLANT POINTS: 5½

200g dried green lentils, rinsed

4 skinless cod fillets (around 140g per fillet)

150g aubergine, chopped

2 tbsp jarred capers, drained

½ red onion, chopped

small handful of torn basil leaves, plus extra to garnish

250g cherry tomatoes

olive oil, for drizzling

1 x 400g tin chopped tomatoes

60g tomato purée

1 tbsp red wine vinegar

salt and pepper

1. Cook the lentils in a large saucepan of simmering water for about 25 minutes, until tender.

2. Preheat the oven to 200°C (180°C fan/400°F) and line a baking tray with baking parchment.

3. Put the cod fillets on the lined baking tray with the aubergine, capers, onion, basil and cherry tomatoes. Drizzle with olive oil and season with salt and pepper (put the cod and vegetables onto 2 separate baking trays if you prefer to cook them separately).

4. Bake the cod and vegetables in the oven on the middle shelf for about 20 minutes, until the cod is cooked through and flakes easily, and the aubergine is tender.

5. When the lentils are cooked, drain them and put them back into the saucepan.

6. After the cod and vegetables are cooked through, remove the tray from the oven and stir all the cooked vegetables into the saucepan with the cooked lentils.

7. Place the pan back over a medium heat, adding the tinned tomatoes, tomato purée and vinegar and stirring well for 3 minutes.

8. Plate up the lentils, placing a cod fillet on top. Season with salt and pepper and garnish with basil leaves.

Easy Chicken Thigh and Roasted Veg Traybake

SERVES 2 • **FIBRE PER SERVING: 10G** • **PLANT POINTS: 5**

4 boneless, skinless chicken thighs

small handful of thyme leaves, chopped

small handful of fresh rosemary leaves

200g aubergine, cut into bite-sized pieces

400g cauliflower, cut into bite-sized pieces

160g Brussels sprouts, halved

For the glaze

1 tsp runny honey

1 tbsp olive oil

3 garlic cloves, finely chopped

juice of ½ lemon

1 tsp Dijon mustard

salt and pepper

1. Preheat the oven to 220°C (200°C fan/425°F) and line a large baking tray with baking paper.

2. Arrange the chicken thighs, herbs and chopped veg on the lined baking tray.

3. Make the glaze by mixing all the ingredients together and seasoning with salt and pepper. Brush the glaze over the chicken thighs and pour the remaining glaze over the rest of the vegetables, coating well and mixing everything with clean hands.

4. Roast in the oven for 30 minutes until the meat is cooked through and the juices run clear when the thighs are pierced with a knife. Remove from the oven and serve hot.

Cauliflower, Coconut and Turmeric Green Curry with Brown Rice

SERVES 4 • **FIBRE PER SERVING: 10G** • PLANT POINTS: 11¼ • VEGAN

280g brown basmati rice, rinsed
generous drizzle of olive oil
1 courgette, cut into chunks
1 large red onion, cut into chunks
300g cauliflower, cut into chunks
70g sugar snap peas
40g spinach leaves
1 x 400g tin butter beans, drained
1 x 400ml tin full-fat coconut milk
55g Thai green curry paste
½ tsp ginger paste
juice of ½ lime

1½ tsp ground turmeric
10g coriander leaves, chopped, plus extra to garnish
handful of torn basil leaves
300ml vegetable stock (I use 1 vegetable stock cube)
¼ tsp garlic powder
½ tsp salt
¼ tsp pepper

To serve
chilli flakes
nigella seeds

1. Put the rice in a medium saucepan and cover with plenty of cold water. Bring to the boil, then reduce the heat and simmer for 20–25 minutes until cooked. Drain well.

2. Heat the oil in a large saucepan over a high heat, add the courgette, onion and cauliflower and fry, stirring regularly, for 3 minutes or until slightly softened. Add the sugar snap peas, spinach and drained butter beans and fry (still over a high heat) for another 2 minutes.

3. Turn the heat down to medium-low and add the coconut milk, curry paste, ginger paste, lime juice, turmeric, coriander, basil leaves, vegetable stock, garlic powder, salt and pepper, and simmer very gently for 10 minutes, until the vegetables are cooked and tender.

4. Serve the rice topped with the curry and extra coriander, sprinkled with chilli flakes and nigella seeds.

Chopped Quinoa and Lentil Salad with Salmon

SERVES 4 • **FIBRE PER SERVING: 10.3G** • **PLANT POINTS: 10**

60g dried red lentils, rinsed

60g quinoa, rinsed

4 salmon fillets (around 520g), skin on

2 tbsp extra virgin olive oil, plus extra for brushing

chilli flakes, to taste, plus extra to serve

1 red onion

80g pitted Kalamata olives

1 red pepper, deseeded

90g sundried tomatoes

½ cucumber

40g rocket

6g fresh parsley leaves, plus extra to garnish

2 tbsp white wine vinegar

180g tinned, drained chickpeas

salt and pepper

1. Put the lentils in a large saucepan of water, bring to the boil, then reduce the heat and simmer for 5 minutes. After 5 minutes add the quinoa to the pan and simmer for another 20 minutes. When the quinoa and lentils are cooked, drain, rinse with cold running water and set aside to cool fully.

2. Preheat the oven to 180°C (160°C fan/350°F).

3. Place the salmon fillets skin side down in an ovenproof dish and brush them with olive oil, crack some pepper over them and lightly sprinkle with chilli flakes. Bake in the oven for 12–14 minutes, or until the salmon is cooked through.

4. As the salmon roasts, prep the vegetables. Dice the onion, olives, red pepper, sundried tomatoes and cucumber and finely chop the rocket and parsley. Place in a large salad bowl and add the 2 tablespoons of olive oil, the vinegar, the chickpeas and the cooked and cooled lentils and quinoa. Season with salt and pepper to taste and mix well.

5. Divide the salad base among four bowls and top with the baked salmon fillets. Garnish with some extra chilli flakes and chopped parsley.

Easy Bean and Veg Stew with Crumbled Feta

SERVES 5 • **FIBRE PER SERVING: 11G** • PLANT POINTS: 8 • VEGGIE

generous drizzle of olive oil

1 large red onion, diced

1 red pepper, deseeded and diced

1 yellow pepper, deseeded and diced

150g celery, diced

150g plum tomatoes, roughly chopped

1 x 400g tin chickpeas, drained

1 x 400g tin black beans, drained

2 x 400g tins chopped tomatoes

4 tbsp tomato purée

1 heaped tbsp nutritional yeast

2 tsp harissa paste

½ tsp garlic powder

1 tsp paprika

large pinch of salt

grind of black pepper

To serve

250g crumbly Greek feta (optional; check it's vegetarian, if necessary)

small bunch of parsley, chopped

5 slices of sourdough bread, toasted (optional)

1. Heat the oil in a large, deep saucepan over a medium-high heat, add the onion, peppers and celery and cook for 3 minutes until softened but not browned. Next, add the chopped plum tomatoes to the pan and cook for 3 more minutes.

2. Add the remaining ingredients, bring to a simmer and cook for 8–10 minutes until everything is tender, then take the saucepan off the heat.

3. Serve each portion topped with 50g crumbled feta (if using), along with some parsley and a drizzle of olive oil. Serve hot, with a slice of toasted sourdough, if you wish.

Tip: This recipe can be made vegan by leaving out the feta cheese as a garnish.

Mexican-inspired Beef and Black Bean Bowls

SERVES 4 • FIBRE PER SERVING: 12.5G • PLANT POINTS: 9¼

drizzle of olive oil

1 red onion, diced

250g lean beef mince

1 tsp garlic powder

1 tsp smoked paprika

2 tbsp tomato purée

1 x 400g tin black beans, drained

1 x 340g tin sweetcorn, drained

salt and pepper

For the guacamole

1½ ripe avocados, peeled and stoned

a pinch of chilli flakes

juice of 1 lime

large pinch of garlic powder

¼ red onion, finely chopped

small handful of coriander, finely chopped

For the salsa

200g plum tomatoes, finely diced

40g red onion, finely diced

½ jalapeño, finely chopped

juice of 1 lime

a few coriander leaves, finely chopped

For the rice

250g brown basmati rice, rinsed

juice of 1 lime

small handful of coriander, finely chopped

1. Make the guacamole: mash the avocado flesh in a bowl, then add the rest of the ingredients, season with salt and pepper and mix well. Set aside.

2. Make the salsa: mix all the ingredients together, season with salt and pepper, then set aside.

3. Put the rice in a large saucepan, cover with cold water, bring to the boil and simmer for 22–25 minutes until cooked.

4. As the rice cooks, fry the beef mince. Heat the olive oil in a saucepan over a medium heat, add the diced onion and sauté for 2 minutes, then add the beef mince, garlic powder and paprika, tomato purée and some salt and pepper and sauté for another 3–4 minutes until the beef mince is browned, breaking it up with a wooden spoon as it cooks. Add the black beans and cook for a further 2 minutes to warm through the beans, then remove from the heat.

5. Drain the cooked rice, add the lime juice and coriander and season with salt. Mix well.

6. Plate up and assemble your Mexican-style bowl, along with the sweetcorn. Enjoy!

Tip: This is easy to make vegan if you swap out the beef mince for Quorn. It will also add another 4g of fibre per serving!

Greek Stuffed Vegetables with Lemon Potatoes

SERVES 4 • FIBRE PER SERVING: 11.7G • PLANT POINTS: 10

2 yellow peppers

2 red peppers

4 large tomatoes

½ courgette

½ aubergine

drizzle of olive oil

½ large white onion, diced

2 garlic cloves, crushed

250g lamb mince

10g dill, chopped

10g mint leaves, chopped

150g brown basmati rice, rinsed

1 x 400g tin chopped tomatoes

2 tbsp tomato purée

1 tbsp white sugar

1 chicken stock cube

100ml warm water

salt

For the lemon potatoes

3 large potatoes, cut into wedges (skin on)

180ml chicken bone broth

juice of 1½ lemons

1 tbsp dried oregano

20ml olive oil

½ tsp garlic powder

1. Put the potato wedges in a large baking dish, pour the bone broth into the dish, then add the lemon juice, a generous pinch of salt, the oregano, olive oil and garlic powder. Mix well to coat and set aside.

2. Preheat the oven to 200°C (180°C fan/400°F).

3. Slice the tops off the peppers and large tomatoes then use a spoon to scoop out the insides, putting the tomato flesh in a separate bowl and discarding the pepper seeds. Keep the tops of these vegetables as you will also use them later as a 'lid' for each one when baking.

4. If the fleshy insides of the tomatoes are in chunks, use a grater to grate them finely so that the tomato insides resemble a sauce.

5. Grate the courgette and aubergine.

6. Heat a drizzle of olive oil in a large saucepan over a medium-high heat. Add the onion and garlic and sauté for a few minutes until softened but not browned then add the lamb mince, grated courgette and aubergine and cook for another 3 minutes, breaking up the lamb mince with a wooden spoon.

7. Add the tomato flesh, chopped dill and mint, rice, half of the tin of tomatoes, the tomato purée, the sugar and another large pinch of salt, then remove from the heat.

8. Spoon this rice and vegetable mixture into the cavity of each empty tomato and pepper, then place them upright in a second baking dish. Place the 'lid' on each one when filled.

9. Add the remaining tinned tomatoes to a blender with the stock cube and warm water, blend well, then pour this into the baking dish around your filled peppers and tomatoes. This will help to keep them nice and moist while in the oven.

10. Bake the potatoes in the oven for 15 minutes, then place the stuffed vegetable dish in the oven and cook both dishes for 1 hour. Halfway through, flip the potato wedges over so that they do not get too dry (and cover the stuffed vegetables with foil if they are browning too quickly).

11. When they are ready, carefully remove from the oven and serve 1 stuffed pepper and 1 stuffed tomato per person, along with a small serving of the lemon potatoes. Spoon the juices from both dishes over the stuffed peppers and potatoes and enjoy!

Tip: To make this vegan, replace the lamb mince with Quorn mince, and use vegetable stock instead of the bone broth and chicken stock.

Lunchtime 5-Veg 'Nourish' Bowl

SERVES 4 • **FIBRE PER SERVING: 15G** • **PLANT POINTS: 13½** • **VEGGIE**

2 medium sweet potatoes, washed and diced (skin on)

1 tbsp extra virgin olive oil

½ tsp paprika

½ tsp cayenne pepper

120g quinoa, rinsed

90g carrot, shredded

100g red cabbage, shredded

120g white cabbage, shredded

30g raisins or sultanas

4 tsp Dijon mustard

4 tsp apple cider vinegar

150ml kefir (or coconut yoghurt, if vegan)

small bunch of dill, fronds chopped

salt and pepper

To serve

2 ripe avocados, peeled and stoned

200g Roasted Red Pepper and Chilli Hummus (page 179)

1. Preheat the oven to 200°C (180°C fan/400°F).

2. Place the diced sweet potatoes on a baking sheet, and coat with the olive oil, ¼ teaspoon of paprika and the cayenne pepper. Season generously with salt and pepper and spread out evenly. Roast in the oven for 20 minutes.

3. Meanwhile, cook the quinoa in a pan of simmering water for 20 minutes, then drain and set aside.

4. Make the slaw by combining the shredded carrot, red and white cabbage, raisins or sultanas, mustard, vinegar, kefir, remaining ¼ teaspoon of paprika, some salt and pepper and the dill in a bowl.

5. Assemble the 'nourish' bowls with the cooked quinoa, the coleslaw, roasted sweet potato, half a sliced avocado per portion and a 50g dollop of hummus.

Tip: This is great for prepping separate salad components ahead of time. The roasted sweet potatoes, cooked quinoa and slaw will keep covered in the fridge for up to 3 days.

11-Plant Pasta

SERVES 4 • **FIBRE PER SERVING: 9.2G** • PLANT POINTS: 11¼

olive oil, for drizzling
1 medium red onion, diced
1 red pepper, deseeded and diced
1½ garlic cloves, crushed
300g wholewheat spaghetti
1 x 400g tin chopped tomatoes
40g pitted Kalamata olives
6g basil leaves, plus extra to serve
10g grated Parmesan cheese or other hard cheese

2 tbsp tomato purée
½ tsp chilli flakes
110g tinned, drained kidney beans
45g walnuts
½ tsp dried oregano
juice of ½ lemon
65g aubergine, roughly chopped
160g chestnut mushrooms, roughly chopped
salt and pepper

1. Heat a drizzle of olive oil in a large saucepan over a high heat, add the onion, red pepper and crushed garlic and fry for 3 minutes, stirring regularly, until softened and lightly browned. Remove from the heat and set aside to cool.

2. As the vegetables cool, bring a separate saucepan of water to the boil. Add the spaghetti and a pinch of salt and cook for 10–12 minutes, or according to the packet instructions.

3. Put the cooled onion, pepper and garlic in a blender along with the chopped tomatoes, olives, basil, Parmesan (if using), tomato purée, chilli flakes, kidney beans, walnuts, oregano, lemon juice and 3 tablespoons of the pasta cooking water from the simmering pasta pan. Blend until smooth and set aside.

4. Heat another drizzle of olive oil in the pan you cooked the vegetables in earlier, over a high heat, add the aubergine and mushrooms and fry for 2 minutes, stirring regularly.

5. After 2 minutes, turn off the heat then pour in the blended sauce you set aside, stirring well to coat the vegetables evenly.

Lamb, Lentil and Sweet Potato Shepherd's Pie

SERVES 6 • **FIBRE PER SERVING: 9.6G** • PLANT POINTS: 9½

800g sweet potatoes, peeled and cut into chunks

drizzle of olive oil

65g celery, diced

1 white onion, diced

1 carrot, diced

100g button mushrooms, sliced

120g frozen peas

220g tinned, drained green lentils

400g lamb mince

½ tsp dried rosemary

½ tsp dried thyme

2 tbsp Worcestershire sauce

3 tbsp tomato purée

1 tsp garlic powder

1 tsp dried parsley

400ml beef stock (I use 1 beef stock cube)

2 bay leaves

2 tbsp nutritional yeast (optional)

50ml whole milk

salt and pepper

1. Cook the sweet potato chunks in a large saucepan of boiling water for about 15 minutes.

2. While the sweet potato cooks, heat a little olive oil in a separate large saucepan over a high heat, add the celery, onion and carrot and cook for 3 minutes, stirring often, until they are soft. After 3 minutes, add the mushrooms, peas and drained lentils and cook for a further 2 minutes.

3. Reduce the heat slightly, add the lamb mince and cook for a few minutes, breaking up the mince with a wooden spoon until it is combined with the vegetables. Add the rosemary, thyme, Worcestershire sauce, tomato purée, garlic powder, parsley, beef stock and bay leaves, stirring well to combine, and season with salt and pepper. Reduce the heat to medium and simmer for 30–35 minutes.

4. When the sweet potatoes are tender, drain and mash with a potato masher, adding the milk, some salt and pepper, and the nutritional yeast (if using). Set aside.

5. Preheat the oven to 190°C (170°C fan/375°F).

6. Remove the bay leaves from the lamb mince and spoon it into a large casserole dish.

7. Carefully top the lamb and vegetables with a thick layer of sweet potato mash, ideally using a piping bag, then bake the shepherd's pie in the oven for 35 minutes.

8. Remove from the oven, carefully spoon into individual dishes and enjoy.

Fibre-fuelled Prawn Stir-fry

SERVES 3 • **FIBRE PER SERVING: 9.5G** • **PLANT POINTS: 11**

160g soba noodles

8g coriander leaves, finely chopped

1 garlic clove, crushed

15g runny honey

10g runny peanut butter

½ red chilli, finely diced, or ¼ tsp chilli flakes

3 tbsp soy sauce

juice of ½ lime

¼ tsp ginger paste

85g frozen edamame beans

½ tsp coconut oil

130g Tenderstem broccoli, cut into bite-sized chunks

90g tinned, drained sweetcorn

50g trimmed cavolo nero or kale, leaves torn into bite-sized pieces

1 red pepper, deseeded and cut into bite-sized chunks

1 yellow pepper, deseeded and cut into bite-sized chunks

15g unsalted peanuts

150g cooked prawns

To serve

1 tsp white sesame seeds

lime wedges

1. Cook the noodles in a pan of boiling water for 4–5 minutes (or according to the packet instructions), until tender. Rinse under cold running water after draining (so they're not too sticky), then drain and set aside.

2. Combine the coriander and garlic in a bowl then add the honey, peanut butter, chilli, soy sauce, lime juice and ginger paste and mix to make the sauce. Set aside.

3. Put the frozen edamame beans in a microwave-safe bowl and add 2 tablespoons of water to the bowl. Microwave the beans for 2 minutes.

4. Heat a wok or large pan over a medium-high heat, add the coconut oil, then add the chopped vegetables, peanuts and prawns, and fry for 4 minutes, stirring regularly.

5. After 4 minutes, add the microwaved edamame beans, the cooked noodles and the sauce you prepared earlier. Stir well to coat everything in the sauce and cook for a further 1 minute, ensuring everything is piping hot.

6. Remove from the heat, divide into 3 portions and serve sprinkled with the sesame seeds, with lime wedges alongside. Enjoy!

Tip: This can be made vegan by replacing the prawns with tofu and the honey with maple syrup.

Snacks

These snack recipes are easy and delicious ways to fuel you while also making it simple to hit your fibre goal for the day! Adding snacks into your regime can help you increase your fibre intake by up to around 20%, while helping to support balanced blood sugar levels throughout the day and helping to reduce hunger levels. Snack options like the Crispy Chickpeas or Kale Crisps may also make great garnishes or additions to salads or soups.

Garlic and Chilli Kale Crisps

SERVES 3 • **FIBRE PER SERVING: 3G** • **PLANT POINTS: 3** • **VEGAN**

180g trimmed curly kale, rinsed

30ml extra virgin olive oil

large pinch of salt

large pinch of cracked black pepper

½ tsp chilli powder (or more if you like it really spicy!)

1 tsp garlic powder

2 tsp white sesame seeds

1. Preheat the oven to 150°C (130°C fan/300°F) and line a large baking tray with baking paper.

2. Lay the kale leaves out on the lined tray.

3. Make the dressing by mixing the olive oil, salt, pepper, chilli powder, garlic and sesame seeds in a bowl. Pour it over the kale leaves on the tray then, using clean hands, mix and coat the kale with the dressing.

4. Bake in the oven on the middle shelf for 25–30 minutes until crispy, checking it regularly and turning the kale leaves over halfway through, ensuring they don't burn.

5. Remove and allow to cool, then serve.

Rosemary, Garlic and Sea Salt Multiseed Crackers

SERVES 6 • **FIBRE PER SERVING: 3.6G** • PLANT POINTS: 5¾ • VEGGIE

25g chia seeds

25g pumpkin seeds

25g sunflower seeds

25g golden linseeds

25g white sesame seeds

120ml room-temperature water

20g runny honey

large pinch of sea salt

some cracked black pepper

1 tbsp finely grated Parmesan or other hard cheese

1 tsp dried rosemary

½ tsp garlic powder

1. Mix all the ingredients in a large bowl until well combined, cover and set aside for about 40 minutes.

2. Preheat the oven to 140°C (120°C fan/275°F) and line a large baking tray with a silicone cooking mat.

3. Once the mixture is ready (it should be sticky), spread it out on the mat quite thinly, to make one large cracker about 37 x 25cm.

4. Bake in the oven on the middle shelf for 45 minutes, then remove and allow to cool on the mat for 15 minutes.

5. Break into slices or large chunks and enjoy on their own, or with a dip such as hummus. The crackers will keep in an airtight container in the cupboard (do not store in the fridge) for up to 1 week.

Crispy Paprika Chickpeas

SERVES 4 • **FIBRE PER SERVING: 4.5G** • **PLANT POINTS: 2** • **VEGAN**

300g tinned, drained chickpeas

1 level tsp garlic powder

¼ tsp salt

1 tsp smoked paprika

½ tsp cracked black pepper

2 tsp extra virgin olive oil

1. Preheat the oven to 220°C (200°C fan/425°F) and line a baking tray with baking paper.

2. Tip the chickpeas onto a clean towel, blot them dry, then tip them into a large bowl. Add the remaining ingredients to the bowl and mix well to coat the chickpeas.

3. Tip the chickpeas onto the lined baking tray, spread out and roast in the oven for 20 minutes, stirring them halfway through.

4. Remove from the oven once they are dried and crispy, then allow to cool before eating.

Easy-prep Fibre-rich Energy Balls

SERVES 4 (2 BALLS PER PORTION) • **FIBRE PER SERVING: 5.7G** •
PLANT POINTS: 6 • VEGGIE

30g pumpkin seeds, finely chopped

30g oat flour (make this yourself by blending oats in the food processor)

20g milled flaxseed

10g chia seeds

40g ground almonds

55g runny almond butter

30g runny honey (or agave syrup, if vegan)

20g 75% dark chocolate (optional)

1. Put all the ingredients (except the dark chocolate, if using) in a mixing bowl and combine well.

2. Using your hands, compress and roll the mixture into 8 small balls and place on a plate.

3. Melt the dark chocolate (see page 182 for melting method), if using, then drizzle it over the energy balls. Place the energy balls in the freezer for 15 minutes, then enjoy. Store in the fridge in an airtight container for up to 7 days.

Sides and Condiments

Adding a side dish can make a big impact on the fibre content of a meal – plus they're a great thing to meal prep in advance on those busy days where you need a fibre boost alongside a protein source. For example, add a side of my Miso Honey Tenderstem Broccoli or Three Bean Salad to an oven-cooked chicken breast or salmon fillet, and you have a super quick and easy lunch. Or, combine these delicious sides alongside the main dishes in this book for an extra fibre hit!

Miso Honey Tenderstem Broccoli

SERVES 4 AS A SIDE • **FIBRE PER SERVING: 3.3G** •
PLANT POINTS: 2¾ • **VEGGIE**

300g Tenderstem broccoli

1 tbsp extra virgin olive oil

30g cashew nuts

1 tsp runny honey

1 tsp white miso paste

½ tsp ginger paste

¼ tsp chilli flakes

1 tbsp water

1. Preheat the oven to 200°C (180°C fan/400°F).

2. Put the Tenderstem broccoli in a baking dish, drizzle with the olive oil and roast in the oven for 20 minutes. After 10 minutes, add the cashew nuts to the dish and return to the oven.

3. Meanwhile, make the sauce by mixing the rest of the ingredients together in a bowl.

4. When the broccoli is tender and the nuts slightly golden, remove from the oven and place in a large bowl. Pour over the sauce, toss well and serve straightaway.

Roasted Beetroot with Crumbled Feta and Thyme

SERVES 4 AS A SIDE • FIBRE PER SERVING: 4.2G •
PLANT POINTS: 1½ • VEGGIE

600g raw beetroot, peeled and cut into chunks

2 tbsp red wine vinegar

1 tbsp extra virgin olive oil

1½ tbsp maple syrup

1 tsp chopped thyme leaves, plus extra to serve

70g crumbly Greek feta cheese (check vegetarian, if necessary)

sea salt flakes

1. Preheat the oven to 220°C (200°C fan/425°F).

2. Put the beetroot chunks in a large ovenproof dish.

3. Mix the vinegar, olive oil, maple syrup and chopped thyme leaves together then pour this mixture over the beetroot. Mix and coat them well.

4. Bake the dressed beetroot in the oven for 50 minutes, turning the beetroot chunks in the dish every 15 minutes or so.

5. Remove from the oven when they are softer and browning at the edges, crumble over the feta cheese, garnish with more thyme leaves and season with sea salt flakes. Serve hot and enjoy.

Artichoke and Rocket Salad

**SERVES 4 AS A SIDE • FIBRE PER SERVING: 3G •
PLANT POINTS: 7½ • VEGGIE**

60g rocket

55g cherry tomatoes, quartered

90g cucumber, halved and sliced

75g tinned, drained chickpeas

115g jarred artichoke hearts

40g red onion, thinly sliced

salt and pepper

For the dressing

1 tsp Dijon mustard

1½ tsp runny honey (or agave syrup, if vegan)

1 tsp white wine vinegar

squeeze of lemon juice

1 tbsp extra virgin olive oil

1. Put all the salad ingredients in a large salad bowl.

2. In a separate small bowl, mix the mustard, honey, vinegar, lemon juice and olive oil to make the dressing.

3. Pour the dressing over the salad, toss well to coat, and serve.

Roasted Red Pepper and Chilli Hummus

SERVES 4 AS A SIDE • FIBRE PER SERVING: 4.7G •
PLANT POINTS: 5 • VEGAN

1 red pepper, deseeded and cut into large chunks

1 tbsp extra virgin olive oil, plus extra to serve

2 tsp white sesame seeds

1 x 400g tin chickpeas, drained (keeping about 3 tbsp liquid from the tin)

½ tsp chilli flakes

juice of ½ lemon

40g tahini

1 large garlic clove

salt and pepper

1. Preheat the oven to 190°C (170°C fan/375°F).

2. Put the chopped pepper on a baking tray, drizzle with the olive oil and season with salt and pepper, and roast in the oven for about 25 minutes.

3. As the pepper roasts, toast the sesame seeds in a dry non-stick frying pan over a medium heat for about 3 minutes, or until golden, moving them around the pan the whole time, then remove from the pan and set aside.

4. Remove the red pepper from the oven and transfer to a plate to cool.

5. Once the red pepper has cooled, add it to a food processor with the remaining ingredients and blend well until smooth. Taste for seasoning and then add some extra salt and pepper, if needed. Serve on a sharing platter, sprinkling the toasted sesame seeds on top and drizzling with more olive oil.

Three Bean Salad

SERVES 4 AS A SIDE • **FIBRE PER SERVING: 6.5G** •
PLANT POINTS: 5¾ • VEGAN

5g fresh dill, finely chopped

5g fresh parsley, finely chopped

½ large red onion, finely diced

75g tinned, drained sweetcorn

110g tinned, drained chickpeas

110g tinned, drained cannellini beans

100g tinned, drained kidney beans

2 tbsp extra virgin olive oil

1½ tbsp white wine vinegar

large pinch of salt

1. Put all the ingredients into a large salad bowl, mix well, serve and enjoy.

High-fibre Raspberry Jam

SERVES 6 • **FIBRE PER SERVING: 3.5G** • PLANT POINTS: 2

200g raspberries
15ml water

25g chia seeds
2 tbsp honey

1. Add the raspberries to a saucepan over a low heat along with the water and cook for 3–4 minutes.

2. As the raspberries heat up and bubble slightly, use a potato masher to mash them so that they become a jam-like consistency. After 3–4 minutes, remove the pan from the heat.

3. Stir the chia seeds and honey into the raspberries and set aside to cool for 10 minutes, still in the saucepan.

4. Transfer the jam to a clean jar or bowl and place in the fridge for at least an hour before serving.

Serving suggestion: Serve with 2 slices of rye bread each to hit 11g of fibre per portion!

Sweet Treats

Eating more fibre doesn't mean having to stick to savoury foods – there are plenty of delicious sweet options that can help fill the fibre gap in your day, too! Dark chocolate is one of my favourite high-fibre ingredients, so you will see it pop up in many of the recipes ahead. These sweet treats show that you do not need to give up anything you love to hit your nutrient goals. Simple swaps like using wholemeal flour can make cakes and loaves higher in fibre while still tasting just as delicious!

Almond Butter-stuffed Dark Chocolate Dates

SERVES 4 (8 DATES TOTAL) • **FIBRE PER SERVING: 3G** •
PLANT POINTS: 3 • **VEGAN**

8 pitted dates

32g almond butter (or peanut butter if you prefer)

35g 75% dark chocolate, broken into pieces (check it's vegan, if necessary)

1. Put the dates on a plate or baking tray lined with baking paper. Open them up slightly and fill each date with some almond butter (about 4g per date).

2. Put the dark chocolate pieces in a large heatproof bowl. Place the bowl over a saucepan of hot water and bring to a simmer (making sure the bottom of the bowl isn't in contact with the water). Melt the dark chocolate gently then remove the bowl from the pan.

3. Using a spoon, drizzle the melted chocolate over each date, to coat it well. Once all the dates are covered with chocolate, place the tray in the freezer for 1 hour.

4. Once frozen, remove and allow to sit for 10 minutes, then enjoy. These can be stored in the freezer for up to 1 month, or the fridge for up to 7 days.

Oat and Almond Dark Choc Chip Cookies

MAKES 8 COOKIES • **FIBRE PER SERVING: 2.8G** •
PLANT POINTS: 3 • VEGGIE

80g oat flour (make this yourself by blending oats in the food processor)

60g ground almonds

1 tsp baking powder

1 large egg

60g coconut oil, melted

100g coconut sugar

60g 75% dark chocolate chips

1. Preheat the oven to 200°C (180°C fan/400°F) and line a baking tray with baking paper.

2. In a large mixing bowl, mix the oat flour, ground almonds and baking powder together evenly. Add the rest of the ingredients and mix well to make the cookie dough.

3. Scoop the dough using a metal spoon and place 8 balls of dough on the lined tray, leaving space between each one. Flatten them into cookies with the back of the spoon and bake in the oven for around 12 minutes until they are brown around the edges but not burnt. They will be soft to touch but will harden once cool.

4. Remove from the oven and allow to cool for 15 minutes on the baking tray before enjoying.

Fibre-boosted Banana Bread

SERVES 9 • **FIBRE PER SERVING: 5.25G** •
PLANT POINTS: 5¼ • VEGGIE

3 ripe bananas

1 tsp baking powder

190g wholemeal flour

70g ground almonds

80g coconut oil, melted

180g coconut sugar

1 tsp vanilla extract

110g 75% dark chocolate chips

1 tsp ground cinnamon

30g runny peanut butter (or any nut or seed butter of your choice)

2 medium eggs

1. Preheat the oven to 180°C (160°C fan/350°F) and line a 2lb loaf tin with baking paper.

2. Mash the bananas in a large mixing bowl until smooth. Combine the baking powder and flour then add them to the mashed bananas with the remaining ingredients and fold together well.

3. Scrape the mixture into the lined tin and level it out. Bake for 1 hour, then test if it's ready by inserting a skewer into the middle of the banana bread. If it comes out clean, it's ready. If there's still raw batter on the skewer, bake it for another 5 minutes then test it again. Remove from the oven, transfer from the tin to a wire rack and allow to cool for 15 minutes before slicing.

4. Slice and serve, on its own or with some Greek yoghurt. The bread will keep for a few days in an airtight container at room temperature.

Beany Dark Chocolate Brownies

MAKES 8 BROWNIES • **FIBRE PER SERVING: 7G** •
PLANT POINTS: 5 • VEGGIE

coconut oil, for greasing

120ml hot water

90g soft pitted dates

300g tinned, rinsed black beans

2 large eggs

2 tbsp dark brown sugar

50g dark cocoa powder

50g ground almonds

50g wholemeal flour

½ tsp baking powder

40g runny honey

60g 75% dark chocolate chips

1. Preheat the oven to 180°C (160°C fan/350°F) and grease a 30 x 20cm brownie tin with coconut oil.

2. Put the hot water and dates in a food processor and blend well until smooth. Add the black beans, eggs, brown sugar and cocoa powder and blend again until smooth.

3. Transfer the mixture to a large mixing bowl and mix in the ground almonds, flour, baking powder, honey and 40g of the dark chocolate chips.

4. Pour the brownie batter into the greased brownie tin, scatter evenly with the remaining 20g dark chocolate chips and bake in the oven on the middle shelf for 25–27 minutes. The brownies can be tested using a skewer, but should be slightly gooey.

5. Remove from the oven carefully and allow to fully cool in the tin before slicing. When cool, slice the brownies in the tin into 8 slices, then carefully remove and place in a large airtight container. Store in the fridge for up to 7 days.

Date and Carrot Cake Slices

SERVES 8 • FIBRE PER SERVING: 6G • PLANT POINTS: 8¾ • VEGAN

200ml plant milk

195g pitted dates

1 ripe banana

100g oat flour (make this yourself by blending oats in the food processor)

100g wholemeal flour

1 tsp ground cinnamon

¼ tsp ground nutmeg

¼ tsp ground ginger

2 tsp baking powder

30g walnuts, finely chopped

15g milled flaxseed

2 eggs

70ml coconut oil, melted

1 medium carrot, peeled and grated

For the glaze

20g maple syrup

15g date syrup

juice of ¼ lemon

¼ tsp ground cinnamon

1 tbsp water

To serve

plain yoghurt

small handful of chopped walnuts

1. Heat the plant milk in a saucepan over a medium-high heat until simmering, then remove from the heat and add the dates. Allow to sit for 30 minutes so the dates soften.

2. Preheat the oven to 180°C (160°C fan/350°F) and line a 30 x 20cm brownie tin with baking parchment.

3. Mash the banana in a large mixing bowl with a fork, until smooth.

4. Add the oat flour, wholemeal flour, spices, baking powder, chopped walnuts, flaxseed, eggs, melted coconut oil and grated carrot to the bowl of mashed banana and stir to thoroughly combine.

5. Once the dates soaking in the milk are soft, add the milk and dates to a food processor or blender and blend well to form a paste. Add the paste to the bowl of other cake ingredients and mix well.

6. Pour the mixture into the lined brownie tin, level it out using a spatula and bake in the oven for 50 minutes.

7. As it cooks, mix all the glaze ingredients together in a bowl. Set aside.

8. Once the cake is ready (you can check using a skewer), remove from the oven and allow it to cool in the tin completely. When it is cooled, pierce some small holes in the top of the cake, then pour half of the glaze on top of it, allowing it to soak it up.

9. Cut the cake into 8 slices and serve each slice with a tablespoon of yoghurt, some crumbled walnuts on top and a drizzle of the remaining glaze. Enjoy!

Dark Chocolate and Avocado Mousse

SERVES 4 • **FIBRE PER SERVING: 7.4G** • PLANT POINTS: 2 • VEGAN

110g 75% dark chocolate, broken into pieces (check it's vegan, if necessary)

15g dark cocoa powder

80ml plant milk

1½ ripe avocados, peeled and stoned

70g maple syrup

1 tsp vanilla extract

1. Put the dark chocolate pieces in a large heatproof bowl. Place the bowl over a saucepan of hot water and bring to a simmer (making sure the bottom of the bowl isn't in contact with the water). Melt the dark chocolate gently, then remove the bowl from the pan.

2. Add the melted dark chocolate and all the remaining ingredients to a food processor and blend well until smooth.

3. Divide the mixture evenly among four ramekins then place them in the freezer for 20 minutes. Remove and enjoy straight away or store in the fridge for up to 2 days.

Meal Plans

To help you get started on your Fibre Fix journey, I have put together some example meal plans using the delicious recipes from the last section. Each day will help you hit 30g of fibre or more. As you will see in the recipe section, most of the main dishes will make 4 servings – enough for you and someone else in your household to enjoy a fibre-filled dish together and then enough for leftovers later in the week, too! This helps reduce time in the kitchen each week and keeps you on track with your fibre goals on those busy days. I have also included an example meal plan to serve one, for those days when you are cooking for yourself (see page 192).

Flexi Meal Plan 1 · Serves 2

Meal	Monday	Tuesday	Wednesday
Breakfast	Warming Apple and Cinnamon Oats (see page 143, double up to serve 2)	5-minute Smoky Baked Beans on Toast (see page 144)	2 pieces of rye bread toast with half a sliced avocado (per person)
Lunch	Lunchtime 5-Veg 'Nourish' Bowl (halve recipe to serve 2, see page 160)	Cod with Tomato and Caper Lentils leftovers (see page 151)	Mexican-inspired Beef and Black Bean Bowls (see page 156)
Dinner	Cod with Tomato and Caper Lentils (see page 151)	Lamb, Lentil and Sweet Potato Shepherd's Pie (see page 162; leftovers are easy to freeze)	11-Plant Pasta (see page 161)
Snack	1 banana (per person)	1 apple (per person)	2 rice cakes with 20g of peanut butter (per person)
Sweet Treats	Almond Butter-stuffed Dark Chocolate Dates (see page 182)	3 squares of 75% dark chocolate (per person)	Date and Carrot Cake Slices (see page 186)
Total Fibre (per person)	41.7g	36g	40.2g

Meat, fish and dairy are all on the table in this delicious weekly meal plan.

Thursday	Friday	Saturday	Sunday
Banana, Chia and Raspberry Pancakes (see page 145)	Courgette Fritters with Poached Egg and Avocado (see page 146)	2 pieces of rye bread toast (per person) with one serving each of High-fibre Raspberry Jam (see page 179)	2 pieces of rye bread toast with 2 scrambled eggs and 100g of baked beans (per person)
Easy Bean and Veg Stew with Crumbled Feta (see page 155)	1 roast chicken breast, mixed salad with rocket leaves and tomato with a side of Roasted Beetroot with Crumbled Feta and Thyme (see page 175)	Easy Bean and Veg Stew with Crumbled Feta leftovers (see page 155) with 1 thick slice of sourdough bread	Chopped Quinoa and Lentil Salad with Salmon (see page 154)
Mexican-inspired Beef and Black Bean Bowls leftovers (see page 156)	Greek Stuffed Vegetables with Lemon Potatoes (see page 158)	11-Plant Pasta leftovers (see page 161)	Easy Bean and Veg Stew with Crumbled Feta leftovers (see page 157) with a side of Artichoke and Rocket Salad (see page 176)
Easy-prep Fibre-rich Energy Balls (see page 171)	Easy-prep Fibre-rich Energy Balls (see page 171)	1 banana (per person)	80g of raspberries (per person)
Almond Butter-stuffed Dark Chocolate Dates leftovers (see page 182)	Date and Carrot Cake Slices leftovers (see page 186)	3 squares of 75% dark chocolate (per person)	1 portion of popcorn (20g)
39g	36.2g	38g	42g

Flexi Meal Plan 2 · Serves 1

Meal	Monday	Tuesday	Wednesday
Breakfast	½ a mashed avocado on 2 pieces of rye bread toast	Warming Apple and Cinnamon Oats (see page 143)	Smoothie: 1 apple, spinach leaves, 1 kiwi, 1 tsp of chia seeds, 1 tsp of manuka honey, half a banana, water
Lunch	1 salmon fillet with Roasted Red Pepper and Chilli Hummus (see page 177) and a portion of Three Bean Salad (see page 179)	Easy Chicken and Veg Traybake (see page 152)	Easy Chicken and Veg Traybake leftovers (see page 152; any leftovers easy to freeze)
Dinner	Cauliflower, Coconut and Turmeric Green Curry with Brown Rice (see page 153)	Creamy Bean and Leek Orzo (see page 150)	Cauliflower, Coconut and Turmeric Green Curry with Brown Rice leftovers (see page 153; any leftovers easy to freeze)
Snack	Small yoghurt bowl with 1 chopped kiwi	Handful of walnuts (20g)	Small bag of popcorn
Sweet Treats	Beany Dark Chocolate Brownie (see page 185)	Oat and Almond Dark Choc Chip Cookie (see page 183)	3 squares of dark chocolate (30g)
Total Fibre (per person)	41.7g	36g	40.2g

This delicious flexitarian meal plan makes life easy when you're solo.

Thursday	Friday	Saturday	Sunday
½ a mashed avocado on 2 pieces of rye bread toast	Warming Apple and Cinnamon Oats (see page 143)	Smoothie: 1 apple, spinach leaves, 1 kiwi, 1 tsp of chia seeds, 1 tsp of manuka honey, half a banana, water	Banana, Chia and Raspberry Pancakes (see page 145)
Fibre-fuelled Prawn Stir-fry (see page 164)	Lunchtime 5-Veg 'Nourish' Bowl (halve recipe to serve 2 and save leftovers, see page 160)	Fibre-fuelled Prawn Stir-fry leftovers (see page 164)	Mexican-inspired Beef and Black Bean Bowls (halve recipe to serve 2 and save leftovers, see page 156)
Creamy Bean and Leek Orzo leftovers (see page 150; any leftovers easy to freeze)	Tuna steak with a side of Miso Honey Tenderstem Broccoli (see page 174) and Artichoke and Rocket Salad (see page 176)	11-Plant Pasta (see page 161)	Easy Chicken and Veg Traybake (see page 152)
Handful of walnuts (20g)	Roasted Red Pepper and Chilli Hummus (see page 177) with carrot sticks	Small yoghurt bowl with 1 chopped kiwi	Roasted Red Pepper and Chilli Hummus leftovers (see page 177) with carrot sticks
Beany Dark Chocolate Brownie leftovers (see page 185)	3 squares of dark chocolate (30g)	Oat and Almond Dark Choc Chip Cookie (see page 183)	Beany Dark Chocolate Brownie (see page 185)
39g	36.2g	38g	42g

Vegetarian Meal Plan · Serves 2

Meal	Monday	Tuesday	Wednesday
Breakfast	Porridge oats (50g) with sliced banana, 1 tbsp chia seeds and honey	Courgette Fritters with Poached Egg and Avocado (see page 146)	2 pieces of wholemeal toast with 2 fried eggs and half an avocado
Lunch	Scrambled tofu (140g) with a side of Miso Honey Tenderstem Broccoli (see page 174) and mixed tomatoes and basil leaves salad	Lunchtime 5-Veg 'Nourish' Bowl (see page 160)	Baked potato filled with sour cream and chives, with a portion of Three Bean Salad (see page 178)
Dinner	Creamy Bean and Leek Orzo (see page 150)	Cauliflower, Coconut and Turmeric Green Curry with Brown Rice (see page 153)	11-Plant Pasta (see page 161)
Snack	Easy-prep Fibre-rich Energy Balls (see page 171)	Garlic and Chilli Kale Crisps (see page 168)	Easy-prep Fibre-rich Energy Balls (see page 171)
Sweet Treats	3 squares of 75% dark chocolate	Almond Butter-stuffed Dark Chocolate Dates (see page 182)	Portion of frozen yoghurt with 10g walnuts, tbsp of sunflower seeds and honey
Total Fibre (per person)	34.7g	39g	37.5g

Thursday	Friday	Saturday	Sunday
Warming Apple and Cinnamon Oats (see page 143)	Courgette Fritters with Poached Egg and Avocado (see page 146)	Green Goddess Shakshuka (see page 142)	Porridge oats (50g) with sliced banana, 1 tbsp chia seeds and honey
Green Goddess Shakshuka (see page 142)	Lunchtime 5-Veg 'Nourish' Bowl leftovers (see page 160)	Scrambled tofu (140g) with a side of Miso Honey Tenderstem Broccoli (see page 174) and mixed tomatoes and basil leaves salad	3-egg omelette with mushrooms, asparagus and portion of Miso Honey Tenderstem Broccoli (see page 174)
Cauliflower, Coconut and Turmeric Green Curry with Brown Rice leftovers (see page 153)	Creamy Bean and Leek Orzo leftovers (see page 150)	11-Plant Pasta leftovers (see page 161)	Easy Bean and Veg Stew with Crumbled Feta (leftovers easy to freeze, see page 155)
Garlic and Chilli Kale Crisps (see page 168)	1 apple	Easy-prep Fibre-rich Energy Balls (see page 171)	2 kiwis
Almond Butter-stuffed Dark Chocolate Dates (see page 182)	3 squares of 75% dark chocolate	Portion of frozen yoghurt with 80g raspberries	Portion of frozen yoghurt with 10g walnuts, tbsp of sunflower seeds and honey
32.7g	36.3g	33.6g	32.6g

MEAL PLANS

Vegan Meal Plan · Serves 2

Meal	Monday	Tuesday	Wednesday
Breakfast	Berry fruit smoothie: 50g each raspberries and blueberries, almond milk, vanilla protein powder, 1 banana, 1 tsp almond butter and ice.	Scrambled tofu (140g) with half an avocado and 1 piece of wholemeal toast	Berry fruit smoothie: 50g each raspberries and blueberries, almond milk, vanilla protein powder, 1 banana, 1 tsp almond butter and ice.
Lunch	Lunchtime 5-Veg 'Nourish' Bowl (replace kefir with coconut yoghurt) (see page 160)	Fibre-fuelled Stir-fry (see Tip on recipe to make it vegan) (see page 164)	Fibre-fuelled Stir-fry (see Tip on recipe to make it vegan) (see page 164)
Dinner	Mexican-inspired Black Bean Bowls (recipe easy to halve, see Tip on recipe to make it vegan page 156)	Greek Stuffed Vegetables with Lemon Potatoes (see Tip on recipe to make it vegan, (see page 158)	Cauliflower, Coconut and Turmeric Green Curry with Brown Rice (see page 153)
Snack	Rosemary, Garlic and Sea Salt Multiseed Crackers (without Parmesan) (see page 169)	Crispy Paprika Chickpeas (see page 170)	Rosemary, Garlic and Sea Salt Multiseed Crackers (without Parmesan) (see page 169)
Sweet Treats	Dark Chocolate and Avocado Mousse (use vegan dark chocolate) (see page 188)	3 squares of vegan dark chocolate	Sweet and salty popcorn
Total Fibre (per person)	50.5g	46.3g	34.1g

Thursday	Friday	Saturday	Sunday
Porridge oats (50g) with sliced banana, 1 tbsp chia seeds and maple syrup	5-minute Smoky Baked Beans on Toast (see page 144)	Scrambled tofu (140g) with half an avocado and 1 piece of wholemeal toast	Porridge oats (50g) with blueberries, 1 tbsp pumpkin seeds and maple syrup
Lunchtime 5-Veg 'Nourish' Bowl (replace kefir with coconut yoghurt) leftovers (see page 160)	Easy Bean and Veg Stew (remove feta) (see page 155)	Baked potato filled with baked beans and vegan cheese, with portion of Three Bean Salad (see page 179)	Easy Bean and Veg Stew (remove feta) leftovers (see page 155)
Greek Stuffed Vegetables with Lemon Potatoes (see Tip on recipe to make it vegan, see page 158)	11-Plant Pasta (remove Parmesan cheese) (see page 161)	Cauliflower, Coconut and Turmeric Green Curry with Brown Rice leftovers (see page 153)	11-Plant Pasta leftovers (see page 161)
Garlic and Chilli Kale Crisps (see page 168)	1 apple	Easy-prep Fibre-rich Energy Balls (see page 171)	2 kiwis
Dark Chocolate and Avocado Mousse (use vegan dark chocolate, see page 188)	Coconut yoghurt with drizzled maple syrup, almonds and dark chocolate chips	3 squares of vegan dark chocolate	Sweet and salty popcorn
53.6g	37.8g	43g	30.9g

Supplements 101

This book is focused primarily on how to get the fibre our bodies need from food. But why haven't I mentioned much about fibre supplements? Well, as a nutritionist, I always have a 'food first' approach when it comes to improving our health and believe that supplements should not be used as a replacement for good dietary habits. It is much better for us to be getting the things we need from whole foods rather than in a synthetic supplement form (unless instructed to do so by our healthcare professional). Fibre supplements are isolated forms of the fibre found in many whole foods, but they do not provide all the additional vitamins, minerals and compounds like antioxidants that whole foods do. In some cases, we see that whole-food sources of fibre are more effective than taking a supplement when it comes to improving our health. For example, in one randomized control trial it was shown that two servings of prunes a day (equalling 6g fibre) was more effective than a psyllium husk supplement (also 6g fibre) when it came to improving stool frequency and consistency in people with constipation[204]. This does not mean that supplements are not useful, it just means that our main focus should be on our diet quality, then we can fill in any gaps with a supplement if we really need one. If you genuinely struggle with consuming enough fibre from whole foods, even after following all the advice outlined in this book, then check out some of the most common fibre supplements below.

Chicory root
Chicory root comes from the chicory plant and is known for its high fibre benefits – with around 90% of its dry weight being made of fibre. The fibre found in chicory root is mostly inulin, but it also contains pectin as well as cellulose. There are some interesting research findings when it comes to how chicory root extracts can help support our health. For example, in one randomized control trial, subjects who consumed raw chicory extract daily for seven weeks saw significant reductions in their total and LDL cholesterol (the bad type of cholesterol)[205]. Other studies show the potential of chicory root to help with weight management[206], improving bowel function while boosting short-chain fatty acids and the beneficial bacteria in our gut[207], as well as even potentially improving insulin sensitivity for individuals with obesity[208].

Chicory root can be taken as a powder form and added to things like coffee, smoothies or food, it can be enjoyed on its own with water (however, it has a bitter taste) or it can be taken as a capsule. Before taking chicory root supplements, it is important to increase your water intake and stay well hydrated to avoid any unwanted symptoms, such as constipation or excess bloating. It is not recommended to take chicory root if you have IBS, are pregnant or breastfeeding, you have gallstones or you have allergies to certain plants like ragweed, daisies or marigolds.

Inulin

Inulin, the main fibre found in chicory root, can be taken as an isolated supplement, too. Inulin in powder form can be added to drinks like your morning coffee, juices or smoothies, or on its own in water. Inulin supplements may improve metabolic function, reduce markers of inflammation, and even improve insulin sensitivity[209] when taken as part of a healthy balanced diet. Inulin supplements have also been shown to make shifts within the gut microbiome – boosting levels of *Anaerostipes*, *Faecalibacterium*, and *Lactobacillus*[210] in the gut, which can contribute to better gut health, digestion and immunity. The typical serving of around 1 teaspoon of inulin powder provides an average of 4–5g of fibre. Like all other fibre supplements, remember to drink enough water if adding them into your routine. If you are on the low-FODMAP diet or have IBS, inulin supplements are not recommended.

Psyllium husk

When mixed with water, psyllium husk forms a sort of 'gloopy'-looking gel. But don't let its texture put you off – psyllium husk is one of the most effective fibre supplements when it comes to improving your gut health, reducing constipation and helping with blood sugar control. One of the most popular ways to use psyllium husk is to mix it with a juice (like cranberry or grape juice), fresh lemon or lime and let it sit for around twenty minutes. It then forms a jelly which can be spread on toast, added to smoothies or protein shakes or even just enjoyed straight from the jar with a spoon! Psyllium husk is considered safe for most people unless you have stomach issues, but it is important to check with your doctor before adding it to your diet.

Psyllium husk jelly recipe: Mix (or blend) 250ml of apple or grape juice with 1 tablespoon of psyllium husk fine powder and the juice of

½ lime. Pour into a jar, cover and allow to sit in the fridge for 20 minutes before enjoying on its own, in smoothies or blended into juices.

Oat bran
Oat bran is rich in the fibre beta-glucan and can help relieve constipation and discomfort as long as it is taken with enough water. In one randomized control trial, an oat bran supplement was also found to be effective in reducing blood pressure in subjects compared to the control group, while also modulating their gut bacteria and reducing their need for drugs used to treat high blood pressure[211]. In another randomized control trial, oat bran showed to be effective in helping people with quiescent ulcerative colitis to keep their symptoms from getting worse, compared to those in the control group[212]. Interestingly, oat bran may also be beneficial in supporting good gut health, particularly after cancer treatment or exposure to radiation. In one animal study, mice who were fed oat bran fibre daily showed that they had less radiation-induced damage to their gut mucous layer, less presence of harmful gut bacteria and more short-chain fatty acids being produced[213]. However, if you are going through radiation therapy it is important to consult with your doctor before making any changes or starting to use a supplement. When taking oat bran as a supplement, you can add it into food or drinks of your choice, or even add it to baked goods to boost the fibre content.

Pectin
The pectin used in pectin supplements usually comes from fruits like apples, pears or citrus fruits. Taking pectin supplements can help to add bulk to your stools, making them easier to pass and helping to prevent constipation[214]. It can also help reduce blood sugar spikes after meals and might even play a role in supporting

mental health. In one pilot study, participants were given a pectin supplement made from citrus fruits and found that it not only helped to reduce inflammatory markers in the body, but it also had an anxiety-reducing effect after four weeks[215]. Pectin can be mixed into drinks or used in baked goods, or as a thickener in cooking. In a 10g serving, you can expect to get around 5g of fibre.

Linseed

Also known as flaxseed, this is a great source of fibre which can help to soften the stool, reduce constipation and support digestive health. Linseed contains mostly insoluble fibre, which passes through the gut without being fermented by gut bacteria. Linseed has been shown to lower cholesterol and increase the amount of fat we excrete[216], potentially helping with weight management, too. I am a big fan of using ground flaxseed supplements in foods like porridge or adding it to a fruit smoothie in the morning to boost the fibre content. I recommend ground over whole flaxseeds, as in this form it can be easier to digest and gentler on your system. One serving (around 20g) contains about 5g of fibre, which is over 15% of what you need in a day.

Before you add any fibre supplements to your diet, check with your doctor or dietitian and ensure that you are drinking enough water. I recommend starting low and slow, building your way up to a full serving of fibre as directed by the packaging. If you begin to get any symptoms like change in stool colour, blood in the stool, painful bloating or other complaints, seek medical help immediately.

Endnotes

1. Scientific Advisory Commission on Nutrition. 'SACN Carbohydrates and Health Report,' Public Health England, TSO 2015.

2. https://pmc.ncbi.nlm.nih.gov/articles/PMC3898422/

3. https://pmc.ncbi.nlm.nih.gov/articles/PMC3213242/

4. https://www.ahajournals.org/doi/10.1161/STROKEAHA.111.000151

5. https://onlinelibrary.wiley.com/doi/10.1111/nbu.12212

6. https://www.amjmed.com/article/S0002-9343(22)00258-3/fulltext

7. https://pubmed.ncbi.nlm.nih.gov/26516908/

8. https://pubmed.ncbi.nlm.nih.gov/31162586/

9. https://pubmed.ncbi.nlm.nih.gov/35125070/

10. https://pmc.ncbi.nlm.nih.gov/articles/PMC12441003/

11. https://www.sciencedirect.com/science/article/pii/S0022316622164503?via%3Dihub

12. https://pubmed.ncbi.nlm.nih.gov/16441938/

13. https://www.sciencedirect.com/science/article/pii/S0268005X-23000413#bbib202

14. https://www.sciencedirect.com/science/article/pii/S0963996925001802

15. https://pmc.ncbi.nlm.nih.gov/articles/PMC3614039/

16. https://academic.oup.com/nutritionreviews/article/78/Supplement_1/78/5877743?login=false

17. https://pubmed.ncbi.nlm.nih.gov/27273067/

18. https://pmc.ncbi.nlm.nih.gov/articles/PMC10302218/

19. https://pubmed.ncbi.nlm.nih.gov/26693746/
20. https://pmc.ncbi.nlm.nih.gov/articles/PMC6352252/
21. https://pubmed.ncbi.nlm.nih.gov/15797686/
22. https://pmc.ncbi.nlm.nih.gov/articles/PMC12277132/
23. https://www.sciencedirect.com/science/article/pii/S0022316622066913
24. https://www.sciencedirect.com/science/article/pii/S0002916522034153
25. https://pubmed.ncbi.nlm.nih.gov/15614200/
26. https://www.nature.com/articles/s41366-018-0093-2
27. https://www.sciencedirect.com/science/article/pii/S0022316622106139
28. https://www.science.org/doi/10.1126/scitranslmed.adm8132
29. https://www.sciencedirect.com/science/article/pii/S1756464616300524?via%3Dihub
30. https://www.sciencedirect.com/science/article/pii/S0002916523036146?ref=cra_js_challenge&fr=RR-1
31. https://www.cambridge.org/core/services/aop-cambridge-core/content/view/5C754A23B955677D57E5305F17F0406E/S0029665113003145a.pdf/dietary-fibre-intake-and-constipation-in-the-uk-womens-cohort-study.pdf
32. https://transform.england.nhs.uk/key-tools-and-info/digital-playbooks/gastroenterology-digital-playbook/remote-monitoring-of-patients-with-small-intestinal-bacterial-overgrowth-IBS-and-food-intolerances/
33. https://aboutibs.org/what-is-ibs/facts-about-ibs/
34. https://5280functionalmed.com/wp-content/uploads/2020/04/The-Effect-of-Fiber-Supplementation-on-Irritable-Bowel-Syndrome-2014.pdf

35 https://bmcpublichealth.biomedcentral.com/artcles/10.1186/1471-2458-14-374

36 https://pmc.ncbi.nlm.nih.gov/articles/PMC4677277/

37 https://pmc.ncbi.nlm.nih.gov/articles/PMC9736284/#:~:text=Dietary%20fiber%20(DF)%2C%20especially,consumption%20of%20carbohydrate%2Drich%20foods.

38 https://pmc.ncbi.nlm.nih.gov/articles/PMC4472947/

39 https://www.mrc-epid.cam.ac.uk/blog/2015/05/27/fibre-risk-diabetes/#:~:text=They%20found%20that%20participants%20with,other%20lifestyle%20and%20dietary%20factors.

40 https://www.cambridge.org/core/journals/british-journal-of-nutrition/article/dietary-fibre-consumption-and-insulin-resistance-the-role-of-body-fat-and-physical-activity/AD0FF04833E5280ACF-3C86A653D6F963

41 https://www.nature.com/articles/s41467-024-46116-y.epdf?sharing_token=JFIltyNhwtw8vhORn5MAD9RgN0jAjWel9jnR3ZoTv0MT0qNg-eYmgMgMvoLzMsrkOos1UX7nLEo6HG6dah608_sjVaBVLPPPOFVWKe-aEVq8zPlh3WCQ_NNIAARP4RlwGZkdF4sgRE9EurK0DdX_kERk0EBF-WtxtAk_v9z6xWRGqk%253D

42 https://www.sciencedirect.com/science/article/pii/S1756464622000561

43 https://www.sciencedirect.com/science/article/pii/S1756464622000561

44 https://www.sciencedirect.com/science/article/pii/S0022316622166903?via%3Dihub

45 https://www.sciencedirect.com/science/article/abs/pii/S1053811919304586

46 https://www.mdpi.com/1422-0067/26/5/2000

47 https://academicmed.org/Uploads/Volume5Issue4/428.%20%5B1391.%20JAMP_Mohamed%20Ali_QR%5D%202127-2130.pdf

48 https://academicmed.org/Uploads/Volume5Issue4/428.%20%5B1391.%20JAMP_Mohamed%20Ali_QR%5D%202127-2130.pdf

49 https://www.jidonline.org/article/S0022-202X(23)01939-5/fulltext

50 https://pmc.ncbi.nlm.nih.gov/articles/PMC10982215/

51 https://pmc.ncbi.nlm.nih.gov/articles/PMC4962284/

52 https://caspjim.com/article-1-2273-en.pdf

53 Gether L, Overgaard LK, Egeberg A, Thyssen JP. Incidence and prevalence of rosacea: a systematic review and meta-analysis. Br J Dermatol 2018 Feb 25

54 https://pmc.ncbi.nlm.nih.gov/articles/PMC11608386/

55 https://www.cochranelibrary.com/cdsr/doi/10.1002/14651858.CD006474.pub3/full

56 https://pubmed.ncbi.nlm.nih.gov/36692989/

57 https://pmc.ncbi.nlm.nih.gov/articles/PMC8264187/#:~:text=Results%3A%20After%20adjustment%20for%20potential,the%20bottom%20quartile%20of%20intake

58 https://www.frontiersin.org/journals/nutrition/articles/10.3389/fnut.2025.1546564/abstract

59 https://pubmed.ncbi.nlm.nih.gov/36692989/

60 https://pubmed.ncbi.nlm.nih.gov/36692989/

61 https://pmc.ncbi.nlm.nih.gov/articles/PMC10205982/

62 https://pubmed.ncbi.nlm.nih.gov/36331819/

63 https://pmc.ncbi.nlm.nih.gov/articles/PMC2744625/#:~:text=Background%3A%20High%2Dfiber%20diets%20have,well%20studied%20in%20premenopausal%20women.

64 https://doi.org/10.3389/fnut.2023.1089891

65 https://doi.org/10.1002/1097-0142(19951215)76:12%3c2491::aid-cncr2820761213%3e3.0.co;2-r

66 https://doi.org/10.1093/ajcn/54.3.520

67 https://www.dietaryguidelines.gov/sites/default/files/2020-12/Dietary_Guidelines_for_Americans_2020-2025.pdf

68 National Diabetes Audit and Scottish Diabetes Survey (2024)

69 Yang Y, Zhao LG, Wu QJ, Ma X, Xiang YB. Association between dietary fiber and lower risk of all-cause mortality: a meta-analysis of cohort studies. Am J Epidemiol 2015;181:-91.
doi: 10.1093/aje/kwu257. pmid: 25552267

70 Veronese N, Solmi M, Caruso MG, etal. Dietary fiber and health outcomes: an umbrella review of systematic reviews and meta-analyses. Am J Clin Nutr 2018;107:-44.
doi: 10.1093/ajcn/nqx082. pmid: 29566200

71 Reynolds A, Mann J, Cummings J, Winter N, Mete E, Te Morenga L. Carbohydrate quality and human health: a series of systematic reviews and meta-analyses. Lancet 2019;393:-45.
doi: 10.1016/S0140-6736(18)31809-9. pmid: 30638909

72 https://www.who.int/data/gho/data/themes/mortality-and-global-health-estimates/ghe-leading-causes-of-death#:~:text=The%20world's%20biggest%20killer%20is,9.0%20million%20deaths%20in%202021.

73 https://www.nature.com/articles/ijo201766

74 https://www.tandfonline.com/doi/full/10.1080/09637486.2018.1446917?needAccess=true

75 https://www.nature.com/articles/ijo201766

76 https://www.thelancet.com/journals/lancet/article/PIIS0140-6736(18)31809-9/fulltext

77 https://pmc.ncbi.nlm.nih.gov/articles/PMC5433529/#:~:text=In%20an%20average%20life%20time,on%20gut%20integrity%20%5B1%5D.

78 https://gutscharity.org.uk/advice-and-information/health-and-lifestyle/introduction-to-gut-bacteria/#:~:text=The%20bacteria%2Fmicroorganisms%20that%20live,same%20as%20an%20adult%20hamster!

79 https://pmc.ncbi.nlm.nih.gov/articles/PMC4480535/

80 https://pmc.ncbi.nlm.nih.gov/articles/PMC10890469/#:~:text=Imbalances%20in%20the%20microbiome%2C%20such,a%20poor%20response%20to%20treatment

81 https://pmc.ncbi.nlm.nih.gov/articles/PMC8733716/

82 https://www.sciencedirect.com/science/article/abs/pii/S027858462030556X?via%3Dihub

83 https://pmc.ncbi.nlm.nih.gov/articles/PMC9504309/

84 https://pmc.ncbi.nlm.nih.gov/articles/PMC10196242/

85 https://pmc.ncbi.nlm.nih.gov/articles/PMC5519041/

86 https://pmc.ncbi.nlm.nih.gov/articles/PMC10133873/

87 https://pubmed.ncbi.nlm.nih.gov/8888921/

88 https://pubmed.ncbi.nlm.nih.gov/32690030/

89 (D'Souza et al., 2017; Parada Venegas et al., 2019).

90 PMID: 30915065

91 https://www.cell.com/cell-metabolism/fulltext/S1550-4131(11)00143-4

92 https://pubmed.ncbi.nlm.nih.gov/22190648/

93 (https://pmc.ncbi.nlm.nih.gov/articles/PMC10180739/)

94 https://www.frontiersin.org/journals/endocrinology/articles/10.3389/fendo.2020.00025/full

95 https://www.sciencedirect.com/science/article/pii/S0303720722000193

96 https://pubmed.ncbi.nlm.nih.gov/31784978/

97 https://pmc.ncbi.nlm.nih.gov/articles/PMC10605799/pdf/40337_2023_Article_917.pdf

98 https://pmc.ncbi.nlm.nih.gov/articles/PMC6187046/

99 https://pubmed.ncbi.nlm.nih.gov/32521538/

100 https://www.cambridge.org/core/journals/british-journal-of-nutrition/article/inulin-oligofructose-and-mineral-metabolism-experimental-data-and-mechanism/095259EB4323F440262F5E-DA67397715

101 Trinidad, P. T., Wolever, T. M. S. & Thompson, L. U. (1993) Interactive effects of Ca and short chain fatty acid on absorption in the distal colon of man. Nutr. Res. 13: 417– 425.

102 https://pmc.ncbi.nlm.nih.gov/articles/PMC6628845/

103 https://pmc.ncbi.nlm.nih.gov/articles/PMC10180739/

104 https://pmc.ncbi.nlm.nih.gov/articles/PMC5131798/

105 https://www.nature.com/articles/nature16504

106 https://pmc.ncbi.nlm.nih.gov/articles/PMC6957715/

107 https://pmc.ncbi.nlm.nih.gov/articles/PMC3742312/

108 https://pmc.ncbi.nlm.nih.gov/articles/PMC3213242/

109 https://pmc.ncbi.nlm.nih.gov/articles/PMC10919761/

110 https://www.frontiersin.org/journals/nutrition/articles/10.3389/fnut.2018.00044/full

111 https://pmc.ncbi.nlm.nih.gov/articles/PMC9528142/

112 Saffarian A, Mulet C, Regnault B, Amiot A, Tran-Van-Nhieu J, Ravel J, et al. Crypt- and mucosa-associated core microbiotas in humans and their alteration in colon cancer patients. mBio. 2019. 10.1128/mBio.01315-19. 10.1128/mBio.01315-19

113 Wu N, Yang X, Zhang R, Li J, Xiao X, Hu Y, et al. Dysbiosis signature of fecal microbiota in colorectal cancer patients. Microb Ecol. 2013;66(2):462–70. 10.1007/s00248-013-0245-9

114 https://pubmed.ncbi.nlm.nih.gov/7576993/

115 https://pmc.ncbi.nlm.nih.gov/articles/PMC6232560/

116 https://pubmed.ncbi.nlm.nih.gov/36606552/

117 https://doi.org/10.1016/j.tifs.2020.04.028

118 https://www.thelancet.com/journals/lancet/article/PIIS0140-6736(17)31363-6/abstract

119 https://pubmed.ncbi.nlm.nih.gov/35125070/

120 https://pmc.ncbi.nlm.nih.gov/articles/PMC11412426/

121 https://www.cdc.gov/heart-disease/data-research/facts-stats/index.html

122 https://www.who.int/europe/news-room/fact-sheets/item/cardiovascular-diseases

123 https://www.sciencedirect.com/science/article/pii/S1875213615001783#:~:text=Accumulating%20evidence%20from%20epidemiological%20studies,intake%20in%20the%20general%20population.

124 https://www.bmj.com/content/348/bmj.g2659

125 https://www.ahajournals.org/doi/10.1161/HYPERTENSIONAHA.123.22575

126 World Health Organization. 2022. Breast cancer. https://www.who.int/news-room/fact-sheets/detail/breast-cancer

127 https://www.cancerresearchuk.org/health-professional/cancer-statistics/statistics-by-cancer-type/breast-cancer

128 https://pmc.ncbi.nlm.nih.gov/articles/PMC10584782/

129 https://www.sciencedirect.com/science/article/pii/S0002916523024553?via%3Dihub

130 https://pubmed.ncbi.nlm.nih.gov/32795218/

131 https://pubmed.ncbi.nlm.nih.gov/22234738/

132 https://pubmed.ncbi.nlm.nih.gov/30670576/

133 https://pubmed.ncbi.nlm.nih.gov/21468064/

134 https://www.sciencedirect.com/science/article/abs/pii/S2212267220315069#:~:text=Sixty%2Dsix%20percent%20of%20studies,met%20their%20national%20fiber%20recommendations.

135 https://pmc.ncbi.nlm.nih.gov/articles/PMC11099360/

136 https://pmc.ncbi.nlm.nih.gov/articles/PMC9017620/

137 *Source: SACN Carbohydrates and Health Report 2015*

138 https://www.kelloggs.co.uk/en_GB/press-release/generation-gut.html

139 https://www.sciencedirect.com/science/article/pii/S2475299124023643

140 *Source: Survey of 2,000 Brits aged 18+, conducted by Censuswide between 16.05.25 and 19.05.25*

141 https://pmc.ncbi.nlm.nih.gov/articles/PMC8746448/

142 https://pmc.ncbi.nlm.nih.gov/articles/PMC8538030/

143 https://nutrition.bmj.com/content/early/2024/01/15/bmjnph-2023-000727

144 https://pubmed.ncbi.nlm.nih.gov/32855515/

145 https://www.medrxiv.org/content/10.1101/2021.05.22.21257615v5

146 https://www.mdpi.com/2072-6643/10/5/587

147 https://www.cambridge.org/core/services/aop-cambridge-core/content/view/F0CFCCC0F985109E1E50B856CE3CC115/S1368980020000518a.pdf/ultra-processed-food-and-beverage-advertising-on-brazilian-television-by-international-network-for-food-and-obesitynon-communicable-diseases-research-monitoring-and-action-support-benchmark.pdf

148 https://pmc.ncbi.nlm.nih.gov/articles/PMC6124841/

149 https://assets.publishing.service.gov.uk/media/5a7f7cc3ed-915d74e622ac2a/SACN_Carbohydrates_and_Health.pdf

150 https://pmc.ncbi.nlm.nih.gov/articles/PMC7987589/

151 https://www.fdf.org.uk/fdf/news-media/news/2022-news/action-on-fibre-working-together/

152 https://www.sciencedirect.com/science/article/abs/pii/

S0963996914000775

153 https://pubmed.ncbi.nlm.nih.gov/23912083/

154 https://pubmed.ncbi.nlm.nih.gov/21468064/

155 https://pubmed.ncbi.nlm.nih.gov/25831134/

156 https://www.sciencedirect.com/science/article/abs/pii/S0091743523003717

157 https://jphe.amegroups.org/article/view/10020/html

158 https://pmc.ncbi.nlm.nih.gov/articles/PMC4408735/

159 https://pubmed.ncbi.nlm.nih.gov/24355537/

160 https://pubmed.ncbi.nlm.nih.gov/24613128/

161 https://pubmed.ncbi.nlm.nih.gov/12449547/

162 https://pubmed.ncbi.nlm.nih.gov/30318190/

163 https://pubmed.ncbi.nlm.nih.gov/26428278/#:~:text=Accordingly%2C%20dietary%20intakes%2C%20anthropometric%20measurements,%C2%B701;%20n%2021).

164 https://pubmed.ncbi.nlm.nih.gov/25109788/

165 https://pubmed.ncbi.nlm.nih.gov/21323688/

166 De Oliveira M.C., Sichieri R., Moura A.S. Weight loss associated with a daily intake of three apples or three pears among overweight women. Nutrition. 2003;19:253–253. doi: 10.1016/s0899-9007(02)00850-x.

167 Brouns F., Theuwissen E., Adam A., Bell M., Berger A., Mensink R.P. Cholesterol-lowering properties of different pectin types in mildly hyper-cholesterolemic men and women. Eur. J. Clin. Nutr. 2012;66:591–599. doi: 10.1038/ejcn.2011.208.

168 https://pubmed.ncbi.nlm.nih.gov/17729399/

169 https://pubmed.ncbi.nlm.nih.gov/12074185/

170 https://pubmed.ncbi.nlm.nih.gov/21147704/

171 https://www.sciencedirect.com/science/article/pii/S0002916522003689

172 https://www.ahajournals.org/doi/10.1161/CIRCULATIONAHA.120.048996

173 https://pmc.ncbi.nlm.nih.gov/articles/PMC10800680/#:~:text=Compared%20with%20never%20consumption%20of,frequencies%20may%20differ%20by%20gender.

174 https://pmc.ncbi.nlm.nih.gov/articles/PMC5086786/

175 https://www.sciencedirect.com/science/article/pii/S000291652204076X#:~:text=Yet%2C%20few%20studies%20have%20specifically,of%20CHD%20in%20other%20studies.

176 https://www.cambridge.org/core/journals/british-journal-of-nutrition/article/different-dietary-fibre-sources-and-risks-of-colorectal-cancer-and-adenoma-a-doseresponse-metaanalysis-of-prospective-studies/BDEA13DC175ACF0B446E5CC0021417FE

177 https://www.gov.uk/government/statistics/ndns-results-from-years-9-to-11-2016-to-2017-and-2018-to-2019

178 https://pubmed.ncbi.nlm.nih.gov/25411276/

179 https://www.nature.com/articles/s41430-021-00875-9

180 https://pmc.ncbi.nlm.nih.gov/articles/PMC5986499/

181 https://www.gov.uk/government/statistics/national-diet-and-nutrition-survey-2019-to-2023/national-diet-and-nutrition-survey-2019-to-2023-report

182 https://pubmed.ncbi.nlm.nih.gov/15228991/

183 https://pmc.ncbi.nlm.nih.gov/articles/PMC6855964/pdf/nmz003.pdf

184 https://pubmed.ncbi.nlm.nih.gov/28392166/

185 https://pmc.ncbi.nlm.nih.gov/articles/PMC4350074/

186 https://www.ncbi.nlm.nih.gov/books/NBK154489/

187 https://link.springer.com/article/10.1007/s13197-016-2391-9

188 https://pmc.ncbi.nlm.nih.gov/articles/PMC10857178/

189 https://pmc.ncbi.nlm.nih.gov/articles/PMC10945126/

190 https://pubmed.ncbi.nlm.nih.gov/30718804/

191 https://www.sciencedirect.com/science/article/abs/pii/S0271531707001066

192 https://www.cambridge.org/core/services/aop-cambridge-core/content/view/73C2B58F9AE6CC08786078548018E30D/S000711450600359Xa.pdf/health-benefits-of-nuts-potential-role-of-antioxidants.pdf

193 https://pmc.ncbi.nlm.nih.gov/articles/PMC9834868/

194 https://pmc.ncbi.nlm.nih.gov/articles/PMC9590345/

195 https://www.mdpi.com/2072-6643/10/2/244#:~:text=5.,prebiotic%20properties%20of%20walnut%20consumption.

196 https://pmc.ncbi.nlm.nih.gov/articles/PMC9861571/

197 https://pmc.ncbi.nlm.nih.gov/articles/PMC12231369/

198 https://assets.publishing.service.gov.uk/government/uploads/system/uploads/attachment_data/file/943114/NDNS_UK_Y9-11_report.pdf

199 https://www.ars.usda.gov/ARSUserFiles/80400530/Pdf/0910/Table_1_Nin_Gen_09.Pdf

200 https://www.sciencedirect.com/science/article/pii/S0965229920318884

201 https://pmc.ncbi.nlm.nih.gov/articles/PMC6916712/

202 https://pmc.ncbi.nlm.nih.gov/articles/PMC8264187/

203 https://www.sciencedirect.com/science/article/abs/pii/S2215036623001931?dgcid=author

204 https://onlinelibrary.wiley.com/doi/abs/10.1111/j.1365-2036.2011.04594.x

205 https://journals.sagepub.com/doi/abs/10.3233/s12349-013-0130-6

206 https://www.sciencedirect.com/science/article/pii/S0002916524007512

207 https://www.cambridge.org/core/journals/gut-microbiome/article/dried-chicory-root-improves-bowel-function-benefits-intestinal-microbial-trophic-chains-and-increases-faecal-and-circulating-short-chain-fatty-acids-in-subjects-at-risk-for-type-2-diabetes/6209AEAFBDDB181197F22AE24388186B

208 https://pubmed.ncbi.nlm.nih.gov/40669445/

209 https://pmc.ncbi.nlm.nih.gov/articles/PMC11397174/

210 https://pubmed.ncbi.nlm.nih.gov/31707507/

211 https://pubmed.ncbi.nlm.nih.gov/34090773/

212 https://pubmed.ncbi.nlm.nih.gov/36777965/

213 https://pubmed.ncbi.nlm.nih.gov/40615440/

214 https://pubmed.ncbi.nlm.nih.gov/35816465/

215 https://pubmed.ncbi.nlm.nih.gov/39408292/

216 https://nutritionandmetabolism.biomedcentral.com/articles/10.1186/1743-7075-9-8

217 https://pmc.ncbi.nlm.nih.gov/articles/PMC10800680/#:~:text=Compared%20with%20never%20consumption%20of,frequencies%20may%20differ%20by%20gender.

218 https://assets.publishing.service.gov.uk/media/5a7f7cc3ed-915d74e622ac2a/SACN_Carbohydrates_and_Health.pdf

219 https://assets.publishing.service.gov.uk/media/5a7f7cc3ed-915d74e622ac2a/SACN_Carbohydrates_and_Health.pdf

Acknowledgements

This book would not have been possible without the support and guidance of so many people.

Firstly, I would like to thank Martha Burley, Managing Editor at Bluebird. Without you, this book would not have been possible. Your belief in me, guidance and constant support has been fundamental to bringing this book to life.

I would also like to thank the rest of the team at Bluebird who have worked tirelessly on getting this book out; the design team for making it look so beautiful, Katy Greenwood and Martha Burley for the editing and re-editing it (even with all of my last-minute changes!), and the comms team, Alexandra Watkins and Elinor Fewster, for helping me get it out into the world.

I would like to thank my soon-to-be-husband Dan. You have been my rock throughout this entire journey – always believing in me, cheering me on and supporting me every step of the way. This book simply would not be what it is without you.

A big thank you to my aunt and uncle, Jackie and David Sinclair who were my true support system throughout my nutrition studies. Without both of you I would not have made it through university and been able to fulfil my dream of becoming an author.

To my mum, who has always taught me to shoot for the stars, believe in yourself and that you can achieve anything you set your mind to. You have made me the person I am today and have been a huge inspiration for writing this book.

And finally, to everyone who has supported my vision and journey to make nutritional information more accessible and easier to understand – especially my social media community who have believed in me, spread the word and cheered me on. This book exists because of you.

Index

A
acne 2, 24–5, 26
Action On Fibre 68
alcohol 38, 49, 75, 134
almonds 80, 83, 114, 115, 116, 129, 171, 184, 196, 197
   Almond Butter-stuffed Dark Chocolate Dates 115, 182, 190, 191, 194, 195
   almond flour 78, 114, 185
   Oat and Almond Dark Choc Chip Cookies 183, 192, 193
Alzheimer's disease 42, 50, 136
American Gut Project 118
American Psychological Association 22
amylase 10
animal foods 62–3, 82, 133
animal studies 24–5, 42, 44, 50, 109, 202
anthocyanins 120
anti-ageing process 23–4, 29
antioxidants 23, 88, 90, 92, 93, 94, 105, 110, 115, 199
anxiety 26, 27, 36, 44, 203
artichokes 55, 85, 93, 95, 104, 105, 129
   Artichoke and Rocket Salad 176, 191, 193
   Jerusalem artichokes 12, 27
asparagus 12, 24, 85, 105, 195

atopic dermatitis 25
autism 41
avocado 4, 21, 55, 79, 84, 92, 93, 97, 103, 156, 160, 190, 192, 193, 196
   Courgette Fritters with Poached Egg and Avocado 146–7, 191, 194, 195
   Dark Chocolate and Avocado Mousse 103, 188, 196, 197

B
B vitamins 39
Bacteroides 17, 43
baked beans 4, 57, 79, 92, 112, 113, 119
   5-Minute Smoky Baked Beans on Toast 144, 190, 197
banana 12, 13, 18, 54, 55, 78, 79, 92, 95, 97, 98, 99, 100, 127, 129, 132, 186, 190–97
   Banana, Chia and Raspberry Pancakes 145, 191
   banana flour 18, 99
   Fibre-boosted Banana Bread 184
beans and legumes 110–13. *See also individual bean, legume and recipe name*
Beany Dark Chocolate Brownies 185, 192, 193

beta-glucans 12, 14, 28, 55, 120
Bifidobacterium 43, 45, 46, 117
bile acids 49
birth delivery 38
bloating 1, 2, 3, 18, 33, 45, 68, 76, 107, 111, 117, 124–9, 134, 200, 203
blood pressure 50, 52–3, 77, 92, 95, 107, 202
blood sugar 13, 20–22, 29, 47, 56, 77, 92, 93, 109, 167, 201
body fat 16, 17
boiling process 126–7
Bowel and Bladder UK 20
brain 7, 39–40, 64
    brain fog 2, 3
    dopamine system 26, 39–40, 64
    gut–brain axis 27, 36, 48, 50
    health 2, 3, 5, 17, 22–3, *23*, 26, 31, 42, 92, 95, 114, 136
    neurotransmitters 36, 39–40
bread 9, 45, 54, 66, 67, 81, 84, 85, 93, 99, 106, 107, 131, 142, 144, 155, 179, 190, 191, 192, 193
    Fibre-boosted Banana Bread 184
    wholegrain 78, 89, 90, 108, 118, 119
breakfast 52, 54, 78, 79, 84, 91, 92, 98, 114
    Banana, Chia and Raspberry Pancakes 145, 191
    Courgette Fritters with Poached Egg and Avocado 146–7, 191, 194, 195
    5-Minute Smoky Baked Beans on Toast 144, 190, 197
    Green Goddess Shakshuka 142, 195
    meal plans 190, 192, 194, 196
    Warming Apple and Cinnamon Oats 143, 190, 192, 193, 195
breast cancer 28, 53–4, 136
Bristol Stool Chart 32
British Nutrition Foundation 66
Broken Plate Report (2025) 61
budget, food 61–3
Burkitt, Denis 'The Fibre Man' 15

C

C-section 38
calories 67, 77, 91, 133
    reduction while boosting fibre 16–17, 18, 84–6
Cambridge University Press 21
cancer. *See individual type of cancer*
Cancer Research UK 53
carbohydrates 3, 9–10, 21, 44, 45, 81, 85, 127, 128
cardiovascular diseases (CVD) 4, 31, 44, 51–3, 94, 99, 107, 109, 136
carotenoids 94, 120
cauliflower 85, 104, 105, 121, 129, 135, 152
Cauliflower, Coconut and Turmeric Green Curry with Brown Rice 153, 194, 195, 196, 197
cell ageing 120

cellulose 12, 14, 120, 200
cereals 49, 51, 66, 78, 87, 92, 107, 114
chia seeds 11, 17, 18, 80, 83, 92, 95, 114, 116, 117, 125, 126, 129, 143, 145, 169, 171, 179, 192–5, 197
chicory root 55, 200–201
cholesterol 4, 12, 13, 33, 52, 92, 101, 109, 113, 117, 136, 200, 203
Chopped Quinoa and Lentil Salad with Salmon 154, 191
Clostridium 43
Cod with Tomato and Caper Lentils 151, 190
cognitive function 22–3, *23*, 29, 35–6, 50, 136
colon 10, 12, 13, 17, 42
cancer 19, 30, 31, 32, 41, 45, 48–50, 53, 66, 101, 105, 110, 136
colorectal cancer 4, 49, 107
constipation 4, 10, 15, 18, 19, 60, 75, 95, 124, 129
    avoiding symptoms of 125–7
    bathroom visits and 33
    cellulose and 12
    chicory root and 200
    cost of 20
    flaxseed and 117, 203
    fruit and 101
    lignins and 13
    oat bran and 202
    pectin and 202
    psyllium husk supplement and 199, 201
cooking process 12, 13, 78, 102, 107, 123, 126–7
Coprococcus eutactus 45
costs
chronic disease 20, 47
    food 61–3, 66, 67, 98, 121
courgette 78, 105, 129, 153, 158, 159
Courgette Fritters with Poached Egg and Avocado 146–7, 191, 194, 195
Creamy Bean and Leek Orzo 150, 192, 193, 194, 195
Crispy Paprika Chickpeas 86, 93, 95, 103, 170, 196
Crohn's disease 25, 41, 46, 55, 98

D

dark chocolate 4, 84, 89, 90, 95, 97, 171, 181, 184
    Almond Butter-stuffed Dark Chocolate Dates 115, 182, 190, 191, 194, 195
    Beany Dark Chocolate Brownies 185, 192, 193
    Dark Chocolate and Avocado Mousse 103, 188, 196, 197
Date and Carrot Cake Slices 186–7, 190, 191
Oat and Almond Dark Choc Chip Cookies 183, 192, 193
delayed gastric emptying 18
dementia 5, 31, 41, 50
depression 26, 27, 44
diarrhoea 57, 127
Dietary Guidelines for Americans 5

digestion
- chewing and 18, 126
- colon cancer and 49
- disorders *see individual disorder name*
- fibre as indigestible part of plants and foods 4, 9, 10, 11, 12, 40
- flaxseed and 117
- gut and 14, 24, 36, 37, 38, 39, 40, 42, 44, 45, 49, 84, 118
- inulin and 201
- kickstarting 3, 17
- lignins and 13
- linseed and 203
- low-fibre days and 134–5
- nuts and seeds and 114
- oligosaccharides and 111
- preparing food and 126–7
- resistant starch and 12
- SCFAs and 42
- water and 126
- weight loss and 17, 18, 19, 21

Disaccharides 9, 128
disease prevention 47–57
- Alzheimer's disease 42, 50, 136
- breast cancer 28, 53–4, 136
- cardiovascular diseases (CVD) 4, 31, 44, 51–3, 94, 99, 107, 109, 136
- colon cancer 19, 30, 31, 32, 41, 45, 48–50, 53, 66, 101, 105, 110, 136
- gut–immune axis 48
- infectious diseases 38, 57
- Inflammatory Bowel Disease (IBD) 25, 41–2, 55–6
- type 2 diabetes 4, 15, 21, 30–31, 44, 53, 56–7, 60, 94, 102, 110

diversifying what you eat 122–3
dopamine 26, 39–40, 64
dose-response relationship 31
'double whammy' foods 82–3
dried foods 21, 62, 66–7, 86, 92, 95, 97, 98, 100, 101, 123, 126, 127, 132–4, 151, 154, 158, 161, 162, 169, 170
drink choices 86

E

E. coli 45
Easy Bean and Veg Stew with Crumbled Feta 123, 155, 191, 195, 197
Easy Chicken Thigh and Roasted Veg Traybake 152
Easy-prep Fibre-rich Energy Balls 171, 191, 194, 195, 197
eat the rainbow 120
eczema 25, 26
edamame beans 81, 83, 84, 94, 111, 112, 113, 122, 164
endometriosis 28
energy levels 3, 9, 20, 21, 92, 109

F

Faecalibacterium prausnitzii 45, 46
false information 67
family, involving in fibre regime 132

fasting and intermittent fasting 2, 77–8
fermentability 11
fibre
    amount of/30g a day 4, 7, 20, 22–3, 27, 28, 30–33, 45, 52, 60, 61, 62, 70, 73–137, 189 *see also* 30g of fibre
    benefits v, 4, 15–33 *see also individual benefit*
    costs and *see* costs
    deficiency crisis 5, 66
    defined 5–6, 9
    digestion and *see* digestion
    disease and *see* disease
    fibremaxxing 69, 87, 91–5
    frustrations 124–9
    gap 5, 87, 181
    getting to know your fibre foods 131–2
    gut and *see* gut
    knowledge gap 59–61
    Kristen Stavridis story with 2–4
    low-fibre days 134
    low-fibre diets 15, 25, 38, 44, 45, 46
    measuring/tracking your intake 32, 74–5
    'nutrient of concern' 7
    prebiotic 12, 14, 24–7
    recipes and meal plans *see* recipes *and* meal plans
    self experiment 5, 45–6
    soluble and insoluble 10–13, 17, 18, 19, 39, 50–52, 55, 75, 86, 87, 107–9, 114, 127, 203
    sources 51, 55, 66–7, 86, 87, 107–108, 114
    supplements *see* supplements
    types 10–13 *see also individual type*
five a day 59, 114
5-Minute Smoky Baked Beans on Toast 144, 190, 197
flaxseed 12, 13, 24, 78, 92, 114, 116, 117, 125, 143, 171, 186, 203
Flexi Meal Plans
    1 190–91
    2 192–3
FODMAPs 128–9, 201
Food and Drink Federation 68
Food and Fiber Summit 68–9
food packaging 91
forever chemicals 28, *29*
free radicals 120
frozen fruit and vegetables 62, 66–7, 98, 120
fruit 12, 19, 21–2, 43, 45, 55, 78, 80, 86, 89, 91, 103, 107, 118–19, 123, 132, 134, 196, 202, 203
    fibre goals and 98–100
    FODMAP and 129
    frozen 62, 66–7, 98, 120
    fruit fibre index 100
    seasonal 63
    skins 10, 88, 102
    sweetening foods with 122

G
GABA 40
Garlic and Chilli Kale Crisps 97,

103, 168, 194, 195, 197
gas, excess 2, 33, 45, 68, 111, 125, 126, 127, 128
gastric cancer 99
gastrointestinal diseases 25
gastrointestinal tract 35, 37
GLP-1 17, 42
glucomannan 26
glycaemic index 24, 93
glycaemic response 21
goals, setting 133
Greek Stuffed Vegetables with Lemon Potatoes 158–9, 191, 196, 197
Green Goddess Shakshuka 142, 195
gums 13, 14
gut
    bacteria 3, 10–14, 17, 24, 27, 31, 37–40, *40*, 42–6, 48–50, 55–6, 84, 92–3, 102, 109, 111, 117, 118, 124, 125, 135, 200, 202, 203
    digestion and 14, 24, 36, 37, 38, 39, 40, 42, 44, 45, 49, 84, 118
    dysbiosis 38
    feelings 35
    gut–brain axis 27, 36, 48, 50
    gut–immune axis 47–9
    gut–skin axis 23–4, 36, 48
    health 2, 3, 4, 11, 12, 23–4, 35–46, 56, 69, 93, 129, 201, 202
    leaky 41, 44
    microbiome 36–8, *40*, 44–6, 48, 55, 57, 77, 95, 109, 118, 122, 124, 130, 201
    microbiome test 45–6

H

Hadza tribe 31
heart health 4, 12, 31, 44, 51–3, 57, 93, 94, 99, 107, 109, 110, 114, 136
heart attack 52
high-volume, low-calorie meals 85
Hippocrates 48
hormones 17, 21, 26, 29, 36, 42, 56, 92, 114
    balance 28
    happy hormones 26, 39
hyperglycaemia 57

I

IBS (irritable bowel syndrome) 19, 25, 101, 105, 127–9, 200, 201
immune system 2, 12, 35–6, 38, 39, 40, 41, 44, 113, 118
    gut–immune axis 47–9
incomplete evacuation 33
inflammation 12, 14, 24, 41, 42, 45, 47, 49, 50, 53, 55, 57, 93, 95, 117, 201
Inflammatory Bowel Disease (IBD) 25, 41–2, 55–6
insoluble fibre 10–13, 19, 55, 127, 203
insulin 21, 56, 93, 200, 201
inulin 12, 14, 24, 26, 27, 86, 200, 201

J
Jam, High-fibre Raspberry 179, 191

K
Kellogg's 60
kitchen, rearranging your 132–3

L
Lactobacillus 45, 201
Lamb, Lentil and Sweet Potato Shepherd's Pie 121, 162–3, 190
leeks 12, 43, 104, 128, 129, 142
    Creamy Bean and Leek Orzo 150, 192, 193, 194, 195
lentils 9, 10, 11, 12, 57, 62, 67, 80, 83, 86, 93, 110, 111, 112, 113, 119, 121, 126, 127, 133
    Chopped Quinoa and Lentil Salad with Salmon 154, 191
    Cod with Tomato and Caper Lentils 151, 190
    Lamb, Lentil and Sweet Potato Shepherd's Pie 121, 162–3, 190
life expectancy 102
lignins 13, 14, 50, 120
linseed 96, 169, 203
longevity 6, 102, 110, 133, 136
'low n' slow' (slowly increasing your fibre intake over time in small amounts) 76–7
lunch 52, 54, 79, 84, 93, 111, 119, 121, 173
    Lunchtime 5-Veg 'Nourish' Bowl 160, 190, 193, 194, 195, 196, 197
meal plans 190, 192, 193, 194, 195, 196, 197

M
main dishes 149–65
    Cauliflower, Coconut and Turmeric Green Curry with Brown Rice 153, 194, 195, 196, 197
    Chopped Quinoa and Lentil Salad with Salmon 154, 191
    Cod with Tomato and Caper Lentils 151, 190
    Creamy Bean and Leek Orzo 150, 192, 193, 194, 195
    Easy Bean and Veg Stew with Crumbled Feta 123, 155, 191, 195, 197
    Easy Chicken Thigh and Roasted Veg Traybake 152
    11-Plant Pasta 102–3, 161, 190, 191, 193, 194, 195, 197
    Fibre-fuelled Prawn Stir-fry 164–5, 193
    Greek Stuffed Vegetables with Lemon Potatoes 158–9, 191, 196, 197
    Lamb, Lentil and Sweet Potato Shepherd's Pie 121, 162–3, 190
    Lunchtime 5-Veg 'Nourish' Bowl 160, 190, 193, 194, 195, 196, 197

Mexican-inspired Beef and
  Black Bean Bowls 123,
  156–7, 190, 191, 193
McDonald's 61
meal plans/meal planning 1, 63,
  79, 130–31, 133, 136, 137, 138,
  189–97
  Flexi Meal Plan 1 190–91
  Flexi Meal Plan 2 192–3
  Vegan Meal Plan 196–7
  Vegetarian Meal Plan 194–5
meal-prepping 123
mental health 2, 3, 4, 26–7, 29,
  35–6, 44, 92, 136, 203
Mexican-inspired Beef and Black
  Bean Bowls 123, 156–7, 190,
  191, 193, 196
Miso Honey Tenderstem Broccoli
  173, 174, 193, 194, 195
monosaccharides 9, 128
MyFitnessPal 67, 74

N

National Diet and Nutrition Survey
  30, 66, 110
neurotransmitters 36, 39–40
norepinephrine 40
nutrient absorption 43
nuts 4, 13, 22, 78, 80, 85–6, 88,
  94, 114–17, 118, 121, 123, 126,
  133–4, 161, 164, 174, 186, 187
  antioxidants and 115
  fibre index 116
  FODMAP foods and 129
  Meal Plans and 192–5

O

oats 108, 109, 114, 119, 126, 127,
  129, 133, 145, 171, 186, 194, 197
Oat and Almond Dark Choc Chip
  Cookies 183, 192, 193
oat bran 202
  Warming Apple and Cinnamon
    Oats 143, 190, 192, 193, 195
Ocado 65
oestrogen 28, 54
oligosaccharides 9, 111, 128
organic food 63
ovulation 2, 3
oxidative stress 24, 117

P

Parkinson's disease 5, 42
pasta 13, 45, 66, 81, 85, 89, 99, 102,
  106, 107, 108, 118, 119, 121
  11-Plant Pasta 102–3, 161, 190,
    191, 193, 194, 195, 197
pectin 11, 14, 19, 50, 95, 101, 120,
  200, 202–3
Peptide YY (PYY) 17, 42
pine nuts 116, 117
pinolenic acid 117
plant foods 3, 4, 5, 9, 10, 11, 12, 54,
  62, 78, 80–85
  bulking up your meals with 121
  experimenting with a more
    plant-based diet 133, 134
  frozen and tinned 120
plant points 114, 118–24, 133 *see
  also individual recipe name*
preparation 126

plate, reshaping 80–86
polysaccharides 9
porridge 17, 21, 52, 78, 92, 114, 121, 143, 194, 195, 197
potatoes 11, 13, 54, 78, 79, 80, 81, 85, 88, 94, 104, 120, 129, 160
    Greek Stuffed Vegetables with Lemon Potatoes 158–9, 191, 196, 197
    Lamb, Lentil and Sweet Potato Shepherd's Pie 121, 162–3, 190
    Prawn Stir-fry, Fibre-fuelled 164–5, 193
prebiotic fibre 12, 14, 24–7
preparing fibre-rich foods 107, 111, 123, 126–7, 130
pressure cooker 127
probiotics 25, 46, 128
protein 3, 17, 21, 24, 45, 62, 65–6, 80, 93, 94, 110, 173, 196, 201
glycoproteins 44
goals 80, 82–4
psoriasis 25
psyllium fibre/psyllium husk 19, 86, 92, 199, 201–2
public health education 59

R

recipe and meal plans 103, 138–98
    breakfast 141–7 *see also* breakfast
    main dishes 148–65 *see also* main dishes
    sides and condiments 172–9 *see also* sides and condiments
    snacks 167–71 *see also* snacks
    sweet treats 180–88 *see also* sweet treats
resistant starch 12–13, 14, 18, 24
rice 9, 13, 51, 52, 67, 78, 81, 84, 85, 89, 94, 97, 106, 107, 108, 109, 118, 119, 131, 133, 190
    Cauliflower, Coconut and Turmeric Green Curry with Brown Rice 153, 192, 194, 195, 196, 197
rinsing foods 126, 127
Roasted Beetroot with Crumbled Feta and Thyme 175, 191
Roasted Mixed Seed Jar 95, 114
Roasted Red Pepper and Chilli Hummus 93, 95, 103, 160, 177, 192, 193
rosacea 25
Rosemary, Garlic and Sea Salt Multiseed Crackers 169, 196
'roughage' 15

S

salads
    Artichoke and Rocket Salad 176, 191, 193
    bags 121
    Chopped Quinoa and Lentil Salad with Salmon 154, 191
    Three Bean Salad 173, 178, 192, 194, 197
sauces 86, 102

hidden veg 121
Scientific Advisory Committee on Nutrition (SACN) 52, 57
sesame seeds 94, 96, 116, 164, 165, 168, 169, 177
seasonal food 63
seeds 80, 86, 118, 119, 121, 122, 123, 129, 133, 134, 135, 158, 168, 169, 171, 177
    chia seeds *see* chia seeds
    flaxseed *see* flaxseed
    Roasted Mixed Seed Jar 95, 114
    sesame seeds *see* sesame seeds
    sunflower seeds *see* sunflower seeds
self experiment 5, 45–6
serotonin 26, 39–40
shopping
    cost 61–3, 67
    diversifying 123
    swaps 89–90, 98
    UPFs 65
short-chain fatty acids (SCFAs) 12, 14, 17, 40–43, *41*, 48, 200, 202
sides and condiments 172–9
    Artichoke and Rocket Salad 176, 191, 193
    High-fibre Raspberry Jam 179, 191
    Miso Honey Tenderstem Broccoli 173, 174, 193, 194, 195
    Roasted Beetroot with Crumbled Feta and Thyme 175, 191
    Roasted Red Pepper and Chilli Hummus 93, 95, 103, 160, 177, 192, 193
    Three Bean Salad 173, 178, 192, 194, 197
Six Steps to 30g 73–137
    fibre frustrations 124–9
    importance of fibre 136–7
    plant points 118–23
    plate, changes to your 80–86
    staying on top of your fibre game 130–35
    what to eat 87–117
    what to know before you start 74–80
skin, human 1, 2, 3, 23–6, *29*, 36, 48, 59, 66, 110, 115, 137
    gut–skin axis 23–4, 36, 48
    microbiome 26
skin, vegetable 10, 78, 88, 102, 104, 114, 116, 143
skipping meals 77–8, 128, 141
sleep 33, 38, 45, 46, 95
small intestine 12, 17, 35, 37
snacks 16, 17, 22, 45, 46, 78, 79, 86, 103, 114, 122, 123, 131–4, 137, 138, 167–71
    Crispy Paprika Chickpeas 86, 93, 95, 103, 170, 196
    Easy-prep Fibre-rich Energy Balls 171, 191, 194, 195, 197
    fibremaxxing and 91, 95–8
    Garlic and Chilli Kale Crisps 97, 103, 168, 194, 195, 197
    Meal Plans 190, 192, 194, 196
    Rosemary, Garlic and Sea Salt Multiseed Crackers 169, 196

swap your snack choices 122
soaking foods 11, 52, 102, 126, 127, 186, 187
social media 4, 16, 67, 69
soluble fibre 10–11, 12, 13, 17, 18, 19, 39, 50, 52, 75, 109
sources of fibre 51, 55, 86, 87, 107–108, 114
low-fibre sources 66–7
spices 119, 121
stress 36, 42–3, 46, 77, 128
stroke 4, 51, 52, 53, 102
sunflower seeds 17, 96, 114, 116, 129, 169, 194, 196
supplements 2, 11, 13, 19, 78, 86, 135, 199–203
   chicory root 200–201
   inulin 201
   linseed 203
   oat bran 202
   pectin 202–3
   psyllium husk 201–2
swaps, food 87, 89–90, 122, 131, 181
sweet treats 103, 114, 181–8, 190, 192, 194, 196
   Almond Butter-stuffed Dark Chocolate Dates 115, 182, 190, 191, 194, 195
   Beany Dark Chocolate Brownies 185, 192, 193
   Dark Chocolate and Avocado Mousse 103, 188, 196, 197
   Date and Carrot Cake Slices 186–7, 190, 191
   Fibre-boosted Banana Bread 184
   Oat and Almond Dark Choc Chip Cookies 183, 192, 193

T

30g fibre a day 4, 7, 20, 22–3, 27, 28, 30–33, 45, 52, 60, 61, 62, 70, 189
   Six Steps to 73–137. *See also* Six Steps to 30g
Three Bean Salad 173, 178, 192, 194, 197
tinned foods 62, 66–7, 120, 121, 127, 142, 144, 151, 154, 159, 161, 162, 164, 170, 176, 178, 185
toxic PFAs (perfluoroalkyl substances) 28
type 2 diabetes 4, 15, 21, 30–31, 44, 53, 56–7, 60, 94, 102, 110

U

ulcerative colitis 41, 44, 45, 55, 202
ultra-processed foods (UPFs) 5, 32, 38, 44, 49, 64–5, 77, 134
unrefined grains, structure of 106, *106*

V

vagus nerve *23*, 36
vegan diet 62, 82
   recipes and 143, 144, 150, 153, 155, 157, 159, 160, 165, 168, 170, 171, 176, 177, 178, 182, 186, 188
Vegan Meal Plan 196–7

vegetables 10, 12, 22, 25, 27, 43, 55,
    61, 67, 78, 102–5
  frozen 62, 66–7, 98, 120
  Greek Stuffed Vegetables with
    Lemon Potatoes 158–9,
    191, 196, 197
  organic 63
  seasonal 63
  skins 10, 78, 88, 102, 104, 114,
    116, 143
  washing 63, 102
vegetarian diet 62 , 82, 134–5, 150,
  155, 175
Vegetarian Meal Plan 194–5
viscosity 11

W

walnuts 116, 117, 171, 161, 186,
  187, 192–5
Warming Apple and Cinnamon Oats
  143, 190, 192, 193, 195
washing fruit and vegetables 63,
  102
water 2, 32, 33, 75–6, 102, 126–8,
  134, 200, 203
weight management 21, 29, 31, 47,
  53, 57, 80, 84–6, 93, 99, 101, 137
  bean and pulses and 113
  calorie reduction while
    boosting fibre 85–6
  chicory root and 200
  fibre as weight-loss hack 16–18
  fruit and 101
  high-volume, low-calorie meals
    85

linseed and 203
low-fibre diet and 1, 2, 3, 5, 7
SCFAs and 42
wholegrain fibre and 109
what to eat 87–117
  beans and legumes 110–13
  fibremaxxing 87, 91–5
  fruit 98–100
  nuts and seeds 114–17
  Roasted Mixed Seed Jar 95, 114
  skins 88
  snacks 97
  swaps, shopping 89–90
  vegetables 102–5
  wholegrains 90, 106–9
wholegrains 4, 25, 43, 49, 51, 52,
  61, 66–7, 80–81, 84, 93, 106–9,
  114, 123, 132, 134–5
  structure of *106*
wholegrain bread 78, 89, 90, 118,
  119
wholegrain fibre index 108–9
women 16, 19, 21, 28, 30, 52, 53,
  110
World Health Organization 31, 48
wrinkles, reducing premature 24–5

younger, looking 1, 23–6, 29